TODAY'S CROCHET

SWEATERS FROM THE CROCHET GUILD OF AMERICA

SUSAN HUXLEY

Martingale™
& COMPANY

Today's Crochet: Sweaters from the Crochet Guild of America
© 2003 by Susan Huxley

Martingale & Company
20205 144th Ave. NE
Woodinville, WA 98072-8478 USA
www.martingale-pub.com

MISSION STATEMENT
DEDICATED TO PROVIDING QUALITY PRODUCTS AND SERVICE TO INSPIRE CREATIVITY.

CREDITS
PRESIDENT: Nancy J. Martin
CEO: Daniel J. Martin
PUBLISHER: Jane Hamada
EDITORIAL DIRECTOR: Mary V. Green
MANAGING EDITOR: Tina Cook
TECHNICAL EDITOR: Ursula Reikes
COPY EDITOR: Liz McGehee
DESIGN DIRECTOR: Stan Green
ILLUSTRATOR: Laurel Strand
COVER PHOTOGRAPHER: Kurt Wilson
COVER DESIGN: Stan Green

CROCHET GUILD OF AMERICA

PO Box 127
Lockport, IL 60441
877-852-9190 (toll free)
www.crochet.org
www.cgoapresents.com

PRODUCED BY THE SEW 'N TELL STUDIO, EASTON, PENNSYLVANIA
MANAGING EDITOR, ACQUISITIONS AND TECHNICAL EDITOR: Susan Huxley
ACQUISITIONS ASSISTANT: Nancy Brown
PROOFREADER: Oli Landwijt
DESIGN, LAYOUT, AND SCHEMATIC ILLUSTRATIONS: Barbara Field
FASHION PHOTOGRAPHER: Kurt Wilson
HAIR AND MAKEUP ARTIST: Colleen Kubrick
FASHION PHOTOGRAPHER (PAGES 34 AND 50): J. P. Hamel
DETAIL PHOTOGRAPHER: Robert Gerheart
Fashion photography shot at the home of Sandy and Roger Paul in Easton, Pennsylvania

Printed in China
09 08 07 06 05 04 03   8 7 6 5 4 3 2 1
Library of Congress Cataloging-in-Publication data available upon request.
ISBN: 1-56477-487-2

The Crochet Guild of America dedicates this book to the memory of our forebears, who diligently preserved their handiwork. Through these samples, their knowledge was passed down from generation to generation. Sample swatches were made to remember the various stitches, stitch patterns, and techniques—a method used as late as the early twentieth century.

I have childhood memories of digging through my own grandma's treasure box of samples. What ecstasy to choose one and have her teach me how to create one of my own!

It is our hope that this book will help others experience and learn new ways to use their skills.

TOSCA J. MARK
CROCHET GUILD OF AMERICA PRESIDENT

CONTENTS

PREFACE

On behalf of the Crochet Guild of America (CGOA), we are proud to present this book of crocheted sweaters, which features garments designed by members of our organization. We've known for a long time that our membership rolls were packed with talent, and this book proves it. Choosing finalists from the hundreds of superb designs that were submitted was a daunting task for the editor and publisher.

This book is a celebration of creativity and community because it is being released on the cusp of the CGOA's tenth anniversary. Years ago, people just like you came together to create a nonprofit organization dedicated to furthering the art and craft of crochet through education, exhibits, and sharing. Members come together at an annual conference each summer and meet regularly through chapters dotted around the United States and Canada. Check out our Web site (www.crochet.org) for a group near you, or ask for information about starting a chapter if there isn't already one in your vicinity. Our official magazine *Crochet!* brings wonderful patterns and articles into members' homes six times a year; plus we have a great lending library, a terrific Web site, and periodic e-newsletters.

We strive to offer as much as possible to those of you in remote settings who don't have access to local yarn stores or teachers. Programs sponsored by the guild include professional development, a master's certificate program, correspondence courses, and a hook collectors' group. Patterns, crochet-friendly yarn, books, and supplies are sold through the licensee www.CGOApresents.com.

We hope you enjoy making the sweaters in this book and that you will join CGOA, to support the work we do and to enrich your own crochet life.

TOSCA J. MARK,
PRESIDENT

JACKIE YOUNG,
VICE PRESIDENT

CINDY COOPER,
TREASURER

BONNIE POLLARD,
SECRETARY

KAREN KLEMP,
PAST PRESIDENT

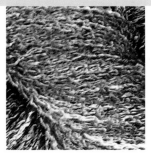

You've fallen in love with a sweater, a stitch pattern that challenges your skills, or perhaps a yarn that begs to be touched. What you want to do—right now—is start crocheting the garment pieces. But read this section first.

It's hard enough suppressing your enthusiasm long enough to make a gauge swatch, let alone work your way through background information you need to know before you pick up a hook. For this reason, the patterns in *Today's Crochet: Sweaters from the Crochet Guild of America* are set up so that you can start stitching as soon as possible.

If crocheting is new to you, take the time to review "Start-Up Strategies for Beginners" on page 72.

Aside from the basic stitches, everything you need to know is presented right in the instructions for each project—there's even a row-by-row explanation of the stitch pattern that you need to work to test the gauge.

YOU'RE GOING

TO HAVE A

GREAT TIME

CROCHETING

YOUR SWEATER!

A quick glance at "Abbreviations" on page 87 will show you that the instructions are written in the traditional language of crochet. Note that the sweater sizing in the project instructions might be a bit different than you're used to because it's based on realistic, up-to-date body measurements. This shouldn't delay you, because every project lists all the body and finished garment measurements you need to pick a sweater size that's perfect for you. Whether your full bust is 31½" or 43¼"—or anywhere in between—there's a set of instructions for you.

Many stitchers falter when they search for the recommended yarn. If it isn't available locally and they don't want to order over the Internet or through a traditional mail-order source, they're stuck trying to find a replacement. Now that's a daunting task. To make it less difficult, every project in this book shows the sweater worked in a specific yarn, but the instructions give you a considerable amount of information to help you select a replacement. A symbol that describes the yarn is placed right on the sweater photo. (See "Yarn Symbols" on the opposite page.) When you look at a sweater you'll immediately know the yarn weight and approximate gauge. On pages 90–91 there's a picture of every yarn strand, shown at its actual size, plus a list of its contents and even the gauge information so that you can compare it with the information on the wrapper of any substitute yarn. Could it be any easier? Yes. On pages 88–89, you can learn to be more confident at swapping yarns by following the advice and formulas for choosing a suitable replacement.

When the yarn is in your hands, the next step is your gauge swatch. Don't skip swatch making, because your sweater won't fit if you have too few or too many stitches to the inch. Some crochet instructions list gauge in a stitch that isn't needed for the sweater. Not so in *Today's Crochet*! In fact, you can learn the stitch pattern at the same time you're making a swatch to check your gauge.

Relax. You don't have to dig through row-by-row instructions to find the stitch pattern. In *Today's Crochet*, the row-by-row guidance to make every stitch pattern has been broken out of the sweater instructions. When you look at a page, you'll immediately know the number of stitches and rows in the repeat, any additional stitches you need to make the pattern work, plus the extra stitches you need in the chain that starts the work.

Need a stitch refresher? Illustrations and step-by-step instructions in "Stitch Primer" on pages 76–78 explain how to make all of the stitches that are needed for any sweater in this book. Then, as you make each garment piece, you can ensure that it's shaping up as planned by comparing the dimensions to those shown on the schematics (line drawings) in the instructions for each sweater.

Once the pieces are stitched, you can take them to a shop for assembly or do it yourself. On page 75 you'll find some of the blocking and stitching techniques that you can use.

Two of the best features in this book are saved for last: an introduction to the talented designers who created the featured sweaters and information about the Crochet Guild of America. The guild is a superb organization that has something for everyone. Beginning crocheters will find support and guidance. Experts can benefit from the camaraderie, contacts, and information that will stretch their skills.

So pick a crocheted sweater that appeals to you, gather your supplies, and start stitching.

YARN SYMBOLS

F FINE WEIGHT
Example: Celebrity
Suitable for hook sizes B/1 to E/4
    (2.5 mm to 3.5 mm)
Short and Sweet *(see page 40)*

L LIGHTWEIGHT
Example: Blithe
Suitable for hook sizes D/3 to F/5
    (3.25 mm to 4 mm)
English Garden *(see page 10)*

M MEDIUM (DK) WEIGHT
Example: Bliss
Suitable for hook sizes E/4 to F/5
    (3.5 mm to 4.5 mm)
Northern Lights *(see page 35)*

B SLUBBED
Example: Ritz
Suitable for crochet hook sizes G/6 to I/9
    (4.25 mm to 5.5 mm)
The Big Easy *(see page 46)*

Z FUZZY
Example: Kid Mohair
Suitable for crochet hook sizes F/5 to H/8
    (4 mm to 5 mm)
Casual Chic *(see page 66)*

SWEATER

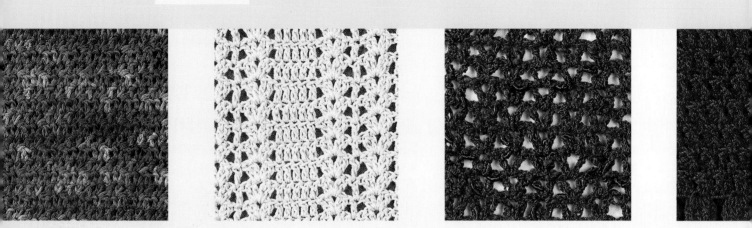

SHOWCASE

English Garden
vest shown in
CGOA Presents
Blithe.

L

ENGLISH GARDEN

BY GWEN BLAKLEY KINSLER, CGOA FOUNDER AND
MEMBER OF THE NORTHERN ILLINOIS CHAPTER

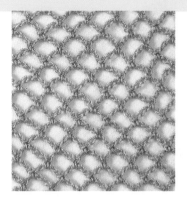

FEATURED STITCHES

Chain (ch); *see page 76*

Chain-space (ch-sp); *see page 80*

Double crochet (dc); *see page 78*

Picot; *see page 82*

Reverse single crochet (rsc); *see page 83*

Single crochet (sc); *see page 77*

Slip stitch (sl st); *see page 77*

Treble crochet (tr); *see page 78*

GAUGE

7 ch-sp and 14 rows to 4" in Trellis
pattern

TOOLS AND SUPPLIES

D/3 (3.25 mm) crochet hook, or size
required to achieve gauge

2 stitch markers

5 (5, 6, 6, 7) buttons, ½" (1.2 cm) wide

6" square of sew-in interfacing or
stabilizer (available in most fabric
and craft stores)

PATTERN POINTERS

The pattern used for the body of this
vest is aptly named because rows of
chain-stitch spaces create a trellis
effect. Worked on a two-row repeat,
the chain-spaces are offset. They are
easy to work and easy to count. For
this reason, the stitch counts at the
end of rows have been replaced with
the number of chain-spaces.

But since the chain-spaces are offset
every second row, the end-of-row
count will be one chain-space less
every second row when the fabric is
worked even. On decrease and
increase rows, the end-of-row chain-
space counts can make it look like
you are working even. But you're not.

Although the rows in the pattern are
different, they look very much alike. At
the beginning of the first row 2, place

Cultivate a casual look with whimsical flowers growing on a crocheted trellis. A soft yarn enhances the unstructured charm.

	SIZE			YARN REQUIREMENTS			*Contrast Colors	
	To fit bust	Finished bust†	Body length	Main color MC (Lilac)	Five contrast colors*		CC1	Dusty pink
EXTRA SMALL	31½"	33¾"	19½"	600 yds. (546 m)	50 yds. (46 m) each color		CC2	Grape (medium purple)
SMALL	34¼"	37"	19½"	800 yds. (728 m)	50 yds. (46 m) each color		CC3	Plum (dark purple)
MEDIUM	37¼"	40¾"	20"	800 yds. (728 m)	50 yds. (46 m) each color		CC4	Seastone (light green)
LARGE	41"	47"	20½"	1,000 yds. (910 m)	50 yds. (46 m) each color		CC5	Jungle (dark green)
FULL FIGURE	43¼"	48¼"	20¾"	1,000 yds. (910 m)	50 yds. (46 m) each color			

†Measurement of buttoned garment

a marker around the turning chain to help you figure out which side of the vest you are working on at any given time as you stitch.

YARN INFORMATION

The English Garden vest is worked in one yarn, CGOA Presents *Blithe* in color #8. Different colors are showcased in the flowers and leaves (#6, #7, #15, #17, and #23), which are sewn on the completed vest. Each flower is worked in a single color (MC, CC1, CC2, or CC3). Two leaves are worked in CC5, one is stitched with CC4. CGOA Presents *Blithe* is a lightweight, medium-twist, cotton-nylon-rayon blend. However, many other yarns are suitable. Gwen suggests Crystal Palace *Baby Georgia* (100% mercerized cotton) and Muench *Roma* (100% mercerized cotton), for example. Pages 88–89 offer guidance on swapping yarns, and pages 90–91 offer additional information about the CGOA Presents yarn.

The yardage chart at the bottom of page 11 tells you the amount of yarn that you need for the main color and five contrast colors. To determine the number of balls you need, divide the amount required, as listed in this chart, by the yardage on the wrapper of the ball or skein that you have decided to use.

TRELLIS PATTERN

Multiple of 3 sts + 2 sts

Foundation Row: Sc in 2nd ch from hk (count as sc), *ch 5, sk next 2 ch, sc in next ch*, rep from * to * to end, turn.

Row 2: Ch 6 (count as sc and ch-sp), sc around first ch-sp, *ch 5, sc around next ch-sp*, rep from * to * to end, ch 3, dc in last sc, turn.

Row 3: Ch 1 (do not count as st), sc in first dc (in same st as ch-1 tch), sk first ch-3 sp and sc, ch 6, sc around next ch-sp, *ch 5, sc around next ch-sp*, rep from * to * to last sc and ch-6 tch, ch 5, sk last sc, sc in 3rd ch of tch, turn.

Next Rows: Rep rows 2 and 3.

BACK

1 With MC, ch 92 (98, 104, 119, 125) loosely.

   Row 1: Sc in 2nd ch from hk (count as sc), *ch 5, sk next 2 ch, sc in next ch*, rep from * to * to end, turn. [30 (32, 34, 39, 41) ch-sp]

2 **Row 2:** Ch 6 (count as st and ch-sp), sc around first ch-5 sp, place marker, *ch 5, sc around next ch-sp*, rep from * to * to last sc, ch 3, dc in last sc, turn. [31 (33, 35, 40, 42) ch-sp]

Row 3: Ch 1, sc in first dc, sk first ch-3 sp and sc, ch 6, sc around next ch-sp, *ch 5, sc in next ch-5 sp*, rep from * to * to last sc and tch, sk last sc, ch 5, sc in 3rd ch of tch, turn. [30 (32, 34, 39, 41) ch-sp]

Trellis pat established.

3 Cont in Trellis pat as established (rep step 2) until 11¼ (11¼, 11¼, 11½, 11½)" from beg, ending with Trellis pat row 3 complete. Fasten off.

ARMHOLE SHAPING

4 **Next Row (Short Row; WS; Trellis Pat Row 2):** Sk first 3 (3, 4, 5, 5) ch-sp, join yarn with sl st in next sc, ch 6, place marker, sc around first ch-sp, *ch 5, sc around next ch-sp*, rep from * to * 22 (24, 24, 27, 29) more times, ch 3, dc in next sc, turn. [25 (27, 27, 30, 32) ch-sp]

5 **Next Row:** Ch 1 (do not count as st), sc in first dc (in same st as ch-1 tch), sk first ch-3 sp and sc, *ch 5, sc in next ch-sp*, rep from * to * to end, working last sc in 3rd ch of 6-ch tch, turn. [24 (26, 26, 29, 31) ch-sp]

6 **Next Row:** Ch 6, sc in first ch-sp, *ch 5, sc in next ch-sp*, rep from * to * to end, ch 3, dc in last sc, turn. [25 (27, 27, 30, 32) ch-sp]

7 Work even in Trellis pat, starting with row 3, until 8 (8, 8½, 8¾, 9)" from beg of armhole shaping, ending with Trellis pat row 2 complete, turn.

RIGHT SHOULDER SHAPING

8 **Next Row:** Rep row 3 of Trellis pat until 6 (7, 7, 8, 8) ch-sp complete, ending with sc in ch-sp, fasten off, then cont with Left Shoulder Shaping. Do not turn.

LEFT SHOULDER SHAPING

9 **Next Row:** Sk 11 (12, 12, 14, 16) ch-sp, join yarn with sc in 3rd ch of next ch-sp, *ch 5, sc in next ch-sp*, rep from * to * to last sc and ch-6 tch, sk last sc, ch 5, sc in 3rd ch of tch. Fasten off. [6 (7, 7, 8, 8) ch-sp]

LEFT FRONT

1 With MC, ch 44 (50, 56, 65, 65) loosely.

Row 1 (RS): As Trellis pat foundation row. [14 (16, 18, 21, 21) ch-sp]

2 **Row 2:** As Trellis pat row 2. [15 (17, 19, 22, 22) ch-sp]

3 **Row 3:** As Trellis pat row 3. [14 (16, 18, 21, 21) ch-sp]

4 Cont in Trellis pat as established until 11¼ (11¼, 11¼, 11½, 11½)" from beg, ending with row 3 complete. Fasten off.

ARMHOLE SHAPING

5 **Next Row (Dec Row; WS):** Sk first 3 (3, 4, 5, 5) ch-sp, join yarn with sl st in next sc, ch 6, place marker, sc around first ch-sp, *ch 5, sc around next ch-sp*, rep from * to * to last sc, ch 3, dc in last sc, turn. [12 (14, 15, 17, 17) ch-sp]

6 **Next Row:** Ch 1 (do not count as st), sc in first dc, sk first ch-3 sp and sc, *ch 5, sc around next ch-sp*, rep from * to * to end, working last sc in 3rd ch of ch-6 sp, turn. [11 (13, 14, 16, 16) ch-sp]

7 **Next Row:** Ch 6, sc in first ch-sp, *ch 5, sc in next ch-sp*, rep from * to * to end, ch 3, dc in last sc, turn. [12 (14, 15, 17, 17) ch-sp]

8 Work even in Trellis pat, starting with row 3, until 2 (2, 2¼, 2½, 2½)" from beg of armhole shaping, ending with Trellis pat row 3 complete, turn. [11 (13, 14, 16, 16) ch-sp]

NECK SHAPING

9 **Next Row (Dec Row):** Ch 6 (count as sc and ch-sp), sc around first ch-sp, *ch 5, sc around next ch-sp*, rep from * to * to end, turn. Rem sc unworked. [11 (13, 14, 16, 16) ch-sp]

10 **Next Row (Dec Row):** Sl st in each of first 3 ch, *ch 5, sc in next ch-sp*, rep from * to *, working last sc in third ch of 6-ch tch, turn. [10 (12, 13, 15, 15) ch-sp]

Next Row (Dec Row): Ch 6, sc in first ch-sp, *ch 5, sc around next ch-sp*, rep from * to * to last ch-sp, ch 5, sl st in third ch of last ch-sp, turn. (Ch-sp count is the same, but a dec has been made.) [10 (12, 13, 15, 15) ch-sp]

11 Rep step 10 for 4 (5, 6, 7, 7) more times, turn. [6 (7, 7, 8, 8) ch-sp]

12 Cont in Trellis pat as established until 8¼ (8¼, 8¾, 9, 9¼)" from beg of armhole. Fasten off.

RIGHT FRONT

1 Work as for Left Front to step 5 (Armhole Shaping), ending with row 2 complete, turn. [15 (17, 19, 22, 22) ch-sp]

ARMHOLE SHAPING

2 **Next Row (Dec Row; RS):** Ch 1 (do not count as st), sc in first dc (in same st as ch-1 tch), sk first ch-3 sp and sc, ch 6, sc around next ch-sp, *ch 5, sc in next ch-sp*, rep from * to * for 8 (10, 11, 13, 13) more times, ch 3, dc in next sc, turn. Rem 4 (4, 5, 6, 6) ch-sp unworked. [11 (13, 14, 16, 16) ch-sp]

3 **Next Row:** As Trellis pat row 2. [11 (13, 14, 16, 16) ch-sp]

4 Cont working even in Trellis pat as established until 2 (2, 2¼, 2½, 2½)" from beg of amhole shaping, ending with Trellis pat row 2 complete, turn. Do not fasten off.

NECK SHAPING

5 **Next Row (Dec Row):** Sk first ch-3 sp and sc, ch 3, sl st in 3rd ch of next ch-sp, *ch 5, sc around next ch-sp*, rep from * to * to last ch-sp, ch 5, sc in 3rd ch of last ch-sp, turn. [10 (12, 13, 15, 15) ch-sp]

Next Row (Dec Row): Ch 6, sc in first ch-sp, *ch 5, sc in next sp*, rep from * to * across, ending with sl st in 3rd ch of last ch-sp, turn. Rem ch-3 sp unworked. [9 (11, 12, 14, 14) ch-sp]

6 Rep step 5 (dec rows) 3 (4, 5, 6, 6) more times. [6 (7, 7, 8, 8) ch-sp]

7 Cont in Trellis pat as established until 8¼ (8¼, 8¾, 9, 9¼)" from beg of armhole. Fasten off.

FINISHING

1 **Shoulder Seam:** With right sides up, butt the top of the left front shoulder against the top of the left back shoulder. Starting at armhole edge, join MC with sc in ch-sp at upper-right corner of back.

2 Sc in same ch-sp on back, ch 2, sc around first ch-sp on front, *ch 2, sc around next ch-sp on back, ch 2, sc around next ch-sp on front*, rep from * to * until all shoulder ch-sps on left front and back are joined, working sc in 3rd ch on last ch-sp on front, ch 2, sc in corresponding sc on back. Fasten off.

3 With MC, join right front shoulder to rem back shoulder in same manner.

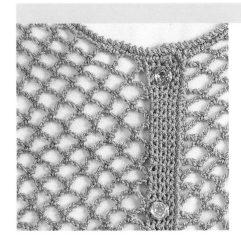

4 **Side Seams:** With MC, join front to back at side seams in same manner as shoulders.

BUTTON BAND

1 Rows are worked into end of each row down left front edge. Attach MC with sl st in first sc in upper right corner.

Row 1: Ch 1, sc in same st as sl st, 2 sc around first tch, sc in next sc, *2 sc around next tch, sc in next sc*, rep from * to * to bottom of front, turn.

2 **Row 2:** Ch 1, sc in first sc and each sc to end, turn.

3 Work even in sc for 3 more rows. Fasten off.

4 Pin-mark the uppermost button position in center of button band, 3 sc from top. Mark start of lowest buttonhole 4 sts from bottom of buttonhole band. Mark 3 (3, 4, 4, 5) more evenly spaced button positions along the button band.

BUTTONHOLE BAND

1 Attach MC with sl st in first sc in lower-right corner of right front.

Row 1: Ch 1, sc in same st as sl st, 2 sc around first dc, sc in next sc, *2 sc around next dc, sc in next sc*, rep from * to * to top of front, turn.

2 **Row 2:** Ch 1, sc in first and each sc to end, turn.

3 Pin-mark buttonhole positions on right front to correspond with button position marks on left front.

4 **Row 3:** Ch 1, sc in first 2 sc, ch 2, sk 2 sc, sc in next sc (buttonhole made), *sc in each sc to mark for next buttonhole, make buttonhole*, rep from * to * to end, turn. (Last buttonhole starts 4 sc from end of row.) [5 (5, 6, 6, 7) buttonholes]

5 **Row 4:** Ch 1, sc in first 2 sc, 2 sc around next ch-2 sp, sc in each sc and around each ch-sp to end, turn.

6 **Row 5:** Ch 1, sc in first sc and each sc to end. Fasten off.

BODY AND NECKLINE EDGING

1 Attach yarn with sl st at bottom of right side seam.

Rnd 1 (Front Hem, RS): Ch 1, sc in same st as sl st, 2 sc around first ch-sp, *sc in available lp of next sc in base ch, 2 sc in next ch-sp*, rep from * to * around edge toward front, 3 sc in lower corner of buttonhole band, pivot, cont with Buttonhole Band.

Buttonhole Band: Sc in end of each row to top, 3 sc in upper corner, pivot, cont with Left Front Neckline.

Left Front Neckline: Sc in end of each row along top edge of buttonhole band, sc in sc at end of buttonhole band, *2 sc in next ch-sp, sc in next sc*, rep from * to * to shoulder, do not turn, cont with Back Neckline.

Back Neckline: Sc in each sc and 2 sc around each ch-sp or dc at end of rows to opposite shoulder, do not turn, cont with Right Front Neckline.

Right Front Neckline: As Body and Neckline Edging rnd 1, Left Front Neckline, ending with sc in edge of each row at top of buttonhole band and 3 sc in corner, pivot, cont with Button Band.

Button Band: As Body and Neckline Edging rnd 1, Buttonhole Band, working down front edge and ending with 3 sc in lower corner, pivot, cont with Rem Hem.

Rem Hem: Sc in end of each row of button band, 2 sc around first ch-sp, *sc in available lp of next sc in base ch, 2 sc in next ch-sp*, rep from * to * around, join to beg of rnd with sl st in first sc at side seam. Do not fasten off. Do not turn.

2 **Rnd 2:** Ch 1, rsc in each sc around, join to beg of rnd with sl st in first sc. Fasten off.

ARMHOLE EDGING

1 With MC, attach yarn with sl st at right underarm seam.

Rnd 1 (RS): Ch 1, sc in side seam, *2 sc around first sp, sc in next sc*, rep from * to * around, join to beg of rnd with sl st in first sc. Do not turn.

2 **Rnd 2:** Ch 1, rsc in first and each sc around, join to beg of rnd with sl st in first sc. Fasten off.

3 Rep edging for left armhole.

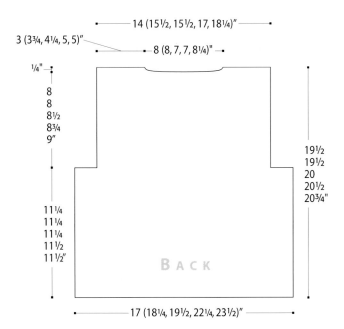

14 (15½, 15½, 17, 18¼)"

3 (3¾, 4¼, 5, 5)"

8 (8, 7, 7, 8¼)"

¼"

8
8
8½
8¾
9"

19½
19½
20
20½
20¾"

11¼
11¼
11¼
11½
11½"

BACK

17 (18¼, 19½, 22¼, 23½)"

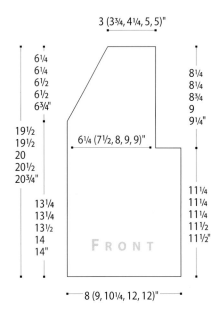

3 (3¾, 4¼, 5, 5)"

6¼
6¼
6½
6½
6¾"

8¼
8¼
8¾
9
9¼"

6¼ (7½, 8, 9, 9)"

19½
19½
20
20½
20¾"

13¼
13¼
13½
14
14"

11¼
11¼
11¼
11½
11½"

FRONT

8 (9, 10¼, 12, 12)"

FLOWER *(Make 4: 1 of each color, as noted in rnd 1.)*

1 **Rnd 1:** With MC, CC1, CC2, or CC3, ch 4, sl st in first ch to form ring.

2 **Rnd 2:** Ch 1, work 10 sc in ring, join to beg of rnd with sl st in first sc. Do not turn.

3 **Rnd 3:** Ch 1, sc in first sc and in each sc around, join to beg of rnd with sl st in first sc. Do not turn.

4 **Rnd 4:** Ch 2 (count as hdc), sk first sc, 2 hdc in each of next 9 sc, hdc in last sc, join to beg of rnd with sl st in top of ch-2 tch. Do not turn.

5 **Rnd 5:** Ch 2, *2 dc in flo in each of next 3 hdc, ch 2, sl st in flo in next hdc*, rep from * to * 4 more times, placing last sl st in same st as base of ch-2 tch at beg of rnd. Do not turn. [5 petals]

6 **Rnd 6:** Working behind each petal of previous rnd and into back lp of each hdc on 3rd rnd, sl st into first hdc, *ch 4, 2 tr in blo of each of next 3 hdc, ch 4, sl st in blo of next

hdc*, rep from * to * 4 more times. Fasten off, leaving long yarn tail for sewing.

LEAF *(Make 3: 1 with CC4 and 2 with CC5.)*

Each leaf is made in a single color. With CC4 or CC5, ch 15.

1 **Foundation Row, Side A:** Sc in 2nd ch from hk (do not count first ch as st), *hdc in next ch, dc in each of next 3 ch, tr in each of next 4 ch, dc in each of next 3 ch, hdc in next ch, sc in next ch, pivot, cont with Foundation Row, Side B. [14 sts]

Foundation Row, Side B: Working in available lps in base ch (working on opposite side of base ch), ch 3 (do not count as st), work from * to * of Foundation Row, Side A. Do not turn. [14 sts]

2 **Rnd 2:** Ch 3 (do not count as st), sc in first sc at beg of Foundation Row, Side A, sc in next hdc, picot, (sc in each of next 2 sts, picot) 6 times, (sc, ch 4, sl st into 3rd ch

from hk, ch 1, sc) around ch-sp at point of leaf, (picot, sc into each of next 2 sts) 7 times, sl st around ch-3 sp. Fasten off, leaving long yarn tail for sewing.

EMBELLISHMENT

1 Arrange flowers and leaves as desired on shoulder. Without attaching pieces to vest, pin them together where they overlap.

2 Cut a piece of stabilizer or interfacing slightly smaller than overall size of grouped flowers and leaves.

3 Pull long yarn tails through flowers and leaves to RS of vest.

4 Place interfacing on WS of vest at shoulder.

5 Pin grouped flowers and leaves on RS of vest to hide interfacing.

6 Using a tapestry needle and yarn tails, sew flowers and leaves to vest, stitching through interfacing for stability.

Endless Summer cardigan and shell shown in CGOA Presents *Tropic.*

L

ENDLESS SUMMER

By Jenny King, CGOA member at large

FEATURED STITCHES

Chain (ch); *see page 76*

Chain-space (ch-sp); *see page 80*

Double crochet (dc); *see page 78*

Double crochet 2 together (dc2tog); *see page 80*

Double crochet in front loop only (dc in flo): *see page 79*

Linked double crochet (ldc); *see page 81*

Single crochet (sc); *see page 77*

Single crochet in back loop only (sc in blo); *see page 79*

Single crochet 2 together (sc2tog); *see page 80*

TOOLS AND SUPPLIES

E/4 (3.5 mm) crochet hook, or size required to achieve gauge

C/2 (3 mm) crochet hook

2 stitch markers (for shell)

GAUGE

Cardigan: 12 ch-sp and 8 rows to 4" in Filet pat with E/4 (3.5 mm) crochet hook

Shell: 24 sts and 14 rows to 4" in ldc with E/4 (3.5 mm) crochet hook

PATTERN POINTERS

The cardigan is a fast and simple garment worked entirely in a filet grid of double crochet and chain stitches. It's trimmed with single crochet edging and does not have an overlapping front closure. The sleeves are worked from the cuff to the shoulder so that you can personalize the fit as you stitch.

The shell, on the other hand, is a bit more complex. It features several stitches, including a variation on the less-known linked double crochet, and innovative shaping. Echoing the openwork cardigan, the lower back alternates rows of filet grid with solid stitching. Below the bra line, this section, which is worked in one piece, shifts into a full-coverage stitch. Shortly thereafter, you work the upper back as 2 separate pieces, with shaping at the inner edges to create the keyhole. Upon its completion, the halves of the upper back are joined

Enjoy blue and green styling from fashion-forward Australian Jenny King. Easy, slim, and sleeveless, the shell features peekaboo back detailing. The counterpoint is a breezy cardigan stitched for oversize ease.

CARDIGAN   SIZES

Note: See page 21 for shell sizes.

YARN REQUIREMENTS

Note: See page 21 for shell yardage.

	To fit bust	Finished bust	Shoulder length	Sleeve length	Body length	Lightweight cotton-acrylic MC1 (Azure)	Lightweight cotton-acrylic MC2 (Turquoise)
EXTRA SMALL	31½"	48"	6"	15"	27½"	1,447 yds. (1,317 m)	200 yds. (182 m)
SMALL	34¼"	50"	7"	15"	28"	1,534 yds. (1,396 m)	200 yds. (182 m)
MEDIUM	37¼"	52"	7½"	15"	29"	1,659 yds. (1,510 m)	200 yds. (182 m)
LARGE	41"	56"	8"	15"	29"	1,765 yds. (1,606 m)	200 yds. (182 m)
FULL FIGURE	43¼"	60"	9"	15"	30"	1,938 yds. (1,764 m)	200 yds. (182 m)

by a length of chain, worked together as a full row, and then separated again for the neckline and shoulder shaping.

YARN INFORMATION

Both the shell and cardigan are worked in a single strand of the same yarn. CGOA Presents *Tropic* is a lightweight, loosely twisted blend of cotton and acrylic. Jenny's playful nature emerges as she chooses 2 different but complementary colors of *Tropic*. The shell's MC is #6 Turquoise with #5 Azure for the contrast. The colorway is reversed for the cardigan.

If you would like to use a different yarn for your garment, test its personality by making a swatch in the featured stitch. The crocheted fabric should drape gently but not be limp. Pages 88–89 offer guidance on swapping yarns. There is additional information about the CGOA Presents yarn on pages 90–91. Suitable replacement yarns for this sweater include Filatura *Brilla* (58% viscose, 42% cotton), Needful Yarns *Kim* (55% cotton, 45% polyester), and Ironstone *Cotton Flake* (100% cotton).

The yardage charts on pages 17 and 21 tell you the amount of yarn that you need. To determine the number of balls, divide the amount required, as listed in this chart, by the yardage on the wrapper of the ball or skein that you have decided to use.

CARDIGAN

FILET PATTERN

Multiple of 2 sts + 1 st (also add 3 sts for base ch)

Foundation Row: Dc in 6th ch from hk (count as dc and ch-sp), *ch 1, sk next ch, dc in next ch (1 ch-sp made)*, rep from * to * to end, turn.

Row 2: Ch 4 (count as dc and ch-sp), sk 1 ch, dc in next dc, *ch 1, sk next ch, dc in next dc*, rep from * to * to end, working last dc in 3rd ch of tch, turn.

Next Rows: Rep row 2.

BACK

1 With larger hk and MC1, ch 148 (154, 160, 172, 184).

Row 1: Dc in 6th ch from hk (count as dc and ch-sp), *ch 1, sk next ch, dc in next ch (1 ch-sp made)*, rep from * to * to end, turn. [72 (75, 78, 84, 90) ch-sp]

2 **Row 2:** Ch 4 (count as dc and ch-sp), sk 1 ch, dc in next dc, *ch 1, sk next ch, dc in next dc*, rep from * to * to end, working last dc in 3rd ch of tch, turn.

Filet pat established.

3 Work even in Filet pat (rep row 2) until 27½ (28, 29, 29, 30)" from beg. Fasten off.

FRONT *(Make 2)*

1 With larger hk and MC1, ch 76 (78, 82, 88, 94).

Row 1: Dc in 6th ch from hk (count as dc and ch-sp), *ch 1, sk next ch, dc in next ch (1 ch-sp made)*, rep from * to * to end, turn. [36 (37, 39, 42, 45) ch-sp]

Row 2: Ch 4 (count as dc and ch-sp), sk 1 ch, dc in next dc, *ch 1, sk next ch, dc in next dc*, rep from * to * to end, working last dc in 3rd ch of tch, turn.

2 Work even in Filet pat (rep row 2) until 14½ (15, 16, 16, 17)" from beg, turn.

NECKLINE SHAPING

3 **Next Row (Dec Row):** Ch 1, sk first dc and ch (dec made at neckline), (sc, ch 2) in next dc (count as dc), place marker, *ch 1, sk 1 ch, dc in next dc*, rep from * to * to end, working last dc in 3rd ch of tch, turn. [35 (36, 38, 41, 44) ch-sp]

Next Row: Ch 4 (count as dc and ch-sp), sk 1 ch, dc in next dc, *ch 1, sk 1 ch, dc in next dc*, rep from * to * to end, working last dc in 2nd ch of tch (with marker), turn.

4 Rep step 3 until 19 (21, 23, 24, 27) ch-sp rem.

Work even in Filet pat until 27½ (28, 29, 29, 30)" from beg. Fasten off.

SLEEVE *(Make 2)*

1 With larger hk and MC1, ch 58 (64, 76, 76, 82).

2 **Row 1:** Dc in 6th ch from hk (count as dc and ch-sp), *ch 1, sk next ch, dc in next ch (1 ch-sp made)*, rep from * to * to end, turn. [27 (30, 36, 36, 39) ch-sp]

Row 2: Ch 4 (count as dc and ch-sp), sk 1 ch, dc in next dc, *ch 1, sk next ch, dc in next dc*, rep from * to * to end, working last dc in 3rd ch of tch, turn.

Work even in Filet pat for 2 more rows.

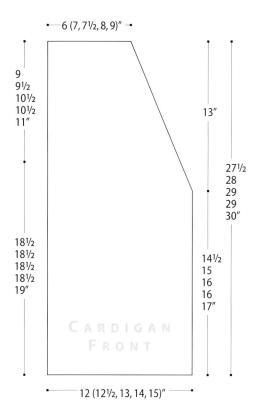

← 6 (7, 7½, 8, 9)" →

9
9½
10½
10½
11"

13"

27½
28
29
29
30"

18½
18½
18½
18½
19"

14½
15
16
16
17"

CARDIGAN
FRONT

← 12 (12½, 13, 14, 15)" →

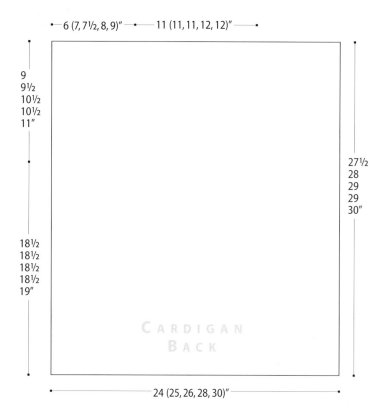

← 6 (7, 7½, 8, 9)" → ← 11 (11, 11, 12, 12)" →

9
9½
10½
10½
11"

27½
28
29
29
30"

18½
18½
18½
18½
19"

CARDIGAN
BACK

← 24 (25, 26, 28, 30)" →

Next Row (Inc Row): Ch 4 (count as dc and ch-sp), (dc, ch 1) in same st as base of ch-4 tch just worked, sk 1 ch, dc in next dc, *ch 1, sk 1 ch, dc in next dc,* rep from * to * to ch-4 tch, ch 1, (dc, ch 1, dc) into 3rd ch of tch, turn. [29 (32, 38, 38, 41) ch-sp]

Rep step 2 until 15" from beg. Fasten off. [55 (58, 64, 64, 67) ch-sp]

FINISHING

If necessary for your yarn, block garment pieces.

With RS tog, sew shoulder seams.

With RS tog, sew sleeves to front and back, placing center of sleeve cap (upper edge) at shoulder seam.

Refold the sweater with front and back RS tog. Starting at sleeve hem, sew sleeve seam, cont sewing along side of body to join front and back.

NECKLINE AND HEM EDGING

With RS facing and smaller hk, attach MC1 with sl st at back of neck.

Rnd 1: Ch 1 (do not count as st), sc in same st, work evenly spaced sc along back (sc around ch-sp, sc in dc), front neckline, and center front opening, 3 sc in corner at bottom of center front, cont evenly spaced sc along hem, 3 sc in corner at bottom of center front, and sc up rem center front, front neckline, and back neckline, join to first ch with sl st. Break yarn. Do not turn.

Rnd 2: With MC2, ch 1 (do not count as st), sc in blo of first sc, sc in blo of each st to first center

← 18 (19, 21, 21, 22)" →

15"

CARDIGAN
SLEEVE

← 9 (10, 12, 12, 13)" →

front lower corner, 3 sc in blo in corner, sc in blo of each st to opposite center front lower corner, 3 sc in blo in corner, sc in each st to end of rnd, join to first ch with sl st. Do not turn. Break yarn.

Attach MC1 and work 2 more rnds of sc in blo, working 3 sc in each lower center front corner. Fasten off.

Endless Summer
shell shown in
CGOA Presents
Tropic.

L

SHELL

See pages 17–18 for "Featured Stitches," "Tools and Supplies," "Gauge," "Pattern Pointers," and "Yarn Information."

AUSSIE OPENWORK PATTERN

Multiple of 2 sts + 1 st (also add 2 sts for base ch)

Foundation Row: Dc in 4th ch from hk (count as 2 dc), dc in next and each ch to end, turn.

Row 2: Ch 4 (count as dc and ch-sp), sk 1 st, dc in next st, *ch 1, sk 1 st, dc in next st*, rep from * to * to end, working last dc in tch, turn.

Row 3: Ch 3 (count as dc), dc around each ch-sp and in each dc to end, dc around tch, dc in 3rd ch of tch, turn.

Next Rows: Rep rows 2 and 3.

LINKED DOUBLE CROCHET PATTERN

Multiple of any number of sts (also add 2 sts for base ch)

Foundation Row: Dc in 4th ch from hk (count as 2 dc), ldc in next and each ch to end, turn.

Row 2: Ch 3 (count as dc), ldc in next and each st to end, turn.

Next Rows: Rep row 2.

FRONT

1 With larger hk and MC2, ch 87 (97, 109, 119, 131).

SLEEVE EDGING

1 With RS facing and smaller hk, attach MC1 with sl st at underarm seam on sleeve hem.

Rnd 1: Ch 1 (do not count as st), sc in same st, work to end in sc, skipping every 2nd ch-sp, join to first ch with sl st. Break yarn. Do not turn.

2 **Rnd 2:** With MC2, ch 1 (do not count as st), sc in blo of first and every st to end of rnd, join to first ch with sl st. Do not turn.

Rnd 3: Ch 1 (do not count as st), sc in blo of first and every st to end of rnd, join to first ch with sl st. Break yarn. Do not turn.

3 **Rnd 4:** With MC1, ch 1 (do not count as st), sc in blo of first and every st to end of rnd, join to first ch with sl st. Do not turn.

Work 1 more rnd of sc in blo. Fasten off.

4 Rep edging for rem armhole.

CARDIGAN STITCHED BY LESTER VAUGHN, MEMBER OF THE CROCHET GUILD OF PUGET SOUND IN WASHINGTON

Row 1: Dc in 4th ch from hk (count as 2 dc), ldc in each ch to end, turn. [85 (95, 107, 117, 129) sts]

Row 2: Ch 3 (count as dc), ldc in flo in next and each st to end, turn.

Rep step 2 twice (work even for 2 rows).

Next Row (Dec Row; RS): Ch 1, sk first st, (sc, ch 1) in next st (dec made, count as 1 st), ldc in next st (linking through lp in sc) and each st across to last 2 sts, dc2tog, turn. [83 (93, 105, 115, 127) sts]

Work even in pat for 3 more rows. Rep step 4 (dec row). [81 (91, 103, 113, 125) sts]

Rep step 5 for 1 (2, 3, 1, 3) more times. [79 (87, 97, 111, 119) sts]

Work even in ldc until 7 (8, 9, 9, 9)" from beg.

Next Row (Inc Row): Ch 3, ldc in same st (base of ch-3 tch), ldc in next and each st to last st, ldc in next and each st to end, turn. [80 (88, 98, 112, 120) sts]

Rep step 8 for 5 more times. [85 (93, 103, 117, 125) sts]

Next Row (Inc Row): Ch 3, ldc in same st (base of ch-3 tch), ldc in next and each st to last st, 2 ldc in last st, turn. [87 (95, 105, 119, 127) sts]

Rep step 10 for 5 more times. [97 (105, 115, 129, 137) sts]

Work even in pat until 11½ (12½, 13½, 13½, 13½)" from beg.

FIRST SHOULDER SHAPING

Next Row: Sl st in first 5 (6, 7, 8, 9) sts, sk 1 st, (sc, ch 1) in next st (count as 1 st), ldc in next and each st to last 7 (8, 9, 10, 11) sts, dc2tog, turn. Rem sts unworked. [85 (91, 99, 111, 117) sts]

Place marker in 43rd (46th, 50th, 56th, 59th) st (center st).

Next Row (Dec Row): Ch 1 (do not count as st), sk 1 st, (sc, ch 1) in next st, ldc in next and each st to last 4 sts before marker, dc2tog twice, turn. [39 (42, 46, 52, 55) sts]

Next Row (Dec Row): Ch 1 (do not count as st), sk first st, (sc, ch 1) in next st (count as 1 st), dc2tog, dc in next and each st to last 2 sts, dc2tog, turn. [36 (39, 43, 49, 52) sts]

Next Row: Ch 3 (count as dc), ldc in next and each st to end, turn.

Next Row (Dec Row): Ch 1 (do not count as st), sk 1 st, (sc, ch 1) in next st (count as 1 st), dc2tog, ldc in next and each st to last 2 sts, dc2tog, turn. [33 (36, 40, 46, 49) sts]

Next Row (Dec Row): Ch 1 (do not count as st), sk first st, (sc, ch 1) in next st (count as 1 st), ldc in next and each st to last 4 sts, dc2tog twice, turn. [30 (33, 37, 43, 46) sts]

Rep step 15 for 1 (2, 2, 2, 2) more times. [18 (13, 13, 19, 22) sts]

Rep first 3 (0, 1, 3, 3) rows of step 15. Fasten off. [9 (9, 10, 10, 13) sts]

SECOND SHOULDER SHAPING

With larger hk, MC2, and working into last full-width row (starting at end of first row of right shoulder shaping), attach yarn with sl st in st with marker.

Next Row (Dec Row): Ch 1 (do not count as st), sk first st, (sc, ch 1) in next st (count as 1 st), dc2tog, dc in next and each st to last 2 sts, dc2tog, turn. [39 (42, 46, 52, 55) sts]

Next Row (Dec Row): Ch 1, sk 1 st, (sc, ch 1) in next st, ldc in next and each st to last 4 sts before marker, dc2tog twice, turn. [36 (39, 43, 49, 52) sts]

Next Row: Ch 3 (count as dc), ldc in next and each st to end, turn.

Next Row (Dec Row): Ch 1, sk 1 st, (sc, ch 1) in next st (count as 1 st), ldc in next and each st to last 4 sts before marker, dc2tog twice, turn. [33 (36, 40, 46, 49) sts]

Next Row (Dec Row): Ch 1 (do not count as st), sk first st, (sc, ch 1) in next st (count as 1 st), dc2tog, ldc in next and each st to last 2 sts, dc2tog, turn. [30 (33, 37, 43, 46) sts]

SHELL	SIZES			YARN REQUIREMENTS	
	Note: See page 17 for cardigan sizes.			**Note:** See page 17 for cardigan yardage.	
	To fit bust	Finished bust	Back length	Lightweight cotton-acrylic MC2 (Turquoise)	Lightweight cotton-acrylic MC1 (Azure)
EXTRA SMALL	31½"	32"	18½"	632 yds. (575 m)	200 yds. (182 m)
SMALL	34¼"	35"	20"	729 yds. (663 m)	200 yds. (182 m)
MEDIUM	37¼"	38"	21½"	836 yds. (761 m)	200 yds. (182 m)
LARGE	41"	42"	22½"	935 yds. (851 m)	200 yds. (182 m)
FULL FIGURE	43¼"	45"	22½"	1,063 yds. (967 m)	200 yds. (182 m)

Next Row: Ch 3 (count as dc), dc in next and each st to end, turn.

20 Rep step 15 for 1 (2, 2, 2, 2) more times. [18 (13, 13, 19, 22) sts]

21 Rep first 3 (0, 1, 3, 3) rows of step 19. Fasten off. [9 (9, 10, 10, 13) sts]

BACK

1 With larger hk and MC2, ch 89 (99, 111, 119, 133).

Row 1: Dc in 4th ch from hk (count as 2 dc), dc in next and each ch to end, turn. [87 (97, 109, 117, 131) sts]

2 **Row 2:** Ch 4 (count as dc and ch-sp), sk first and next st, dc in next st, *ch 1, sk 1 st, dc in next st*, rep from * to * to end, working last dc in tch, turn. [43 (48, 54, 58, 65) ch-sp]

Aussie Openwork pat established.

3 **Row 3:** Ch 3 (count as dc), dc around each ch-sp and in each dc to end, dc around tch, dc in 3rd ch of tch, turn. [87 (97, 109, 117, 131) sts]

4 Rep step 2 once. [43 (48, 54, 58, 65) ch-sp]

Row 5 (Dec Row): Ch 1 (do not count as st), sk first dc, (sc, ch 1) in first ch-sp (count as 1 dc), *dc in next dc, dc around next ch-sp*, rep from * to * to tch, dc in 4th ch of tch, turn. [85 (95, 107, 115, 129) sts]

5 Rep step 4 for 3 (4, 5, 2, 4) more times. [79 (87, 97, 111, 121) sts]

6 Work even in Aussie Openwork pat as established until 7 (8, 9, 9, 9)" from beg.

7 **Next Row (Inc Row):** Ch 3, ldc in same st (base of ch-3 tch), ldc in flo in next and each st to last st, 2 ldc in last st, turn. [81 (89, 99, 113, 123) sts]

8 Rep step 7 for 7 more times. [95 (103, 113, 127, 137) sts]

FIRST UPPER BACK AND SHOULDER

9 **Keyhole Placement:** Place marker on 33rd (36th, 40th, 46th, 51st) and on 63rd (68th, 74th, 82nd, 87th) sts.

10 **Short Row:** Sl st over first 7 (8, 9, 10, 11) sts (armhole edge), ch 3 (count as dc), ldc in next and each st to first marker (do not work in marked st), turn. Rem sts unworked. [26 (28, 31, 36, 40) sts]

11 **Next Row (Dec Row):** Ch 3 (count as dc), ldc in next and each st to last 4 sts, dc2tog, turn. [25 (27, 30, 35, 39) sts]

Next Row (Dec Row): Ch 1 (do not count as st), sk first st, (sc, ch 1) in next st (count as 1 st), ldc in next and each st to end, turn. [24 (26, 29, 34, 38) sts]

12 Rep step 11 for 2 more times. [20 (22, 25, 30, 34) sts]

13 Work even in ldc until 3" from beg of first upper back and shoulder (beg of keyhole).

TOP OF KEYHOLE

14 **Next Row (Inc Row):** Ch 3 (count as dc), ldc in same st (base of ch-3 tch), ldc in next and each st to end, turn. [21 (23, 26, 31, 35) sts]

Next Row (Inc Row): Ch 3 (count as dc), ldc in next and each st to last st, 2 ldc in last st, turn. [22 (24, 27, 32, 36) sts]

15 Rep last 2 rows for 2 more times, do not turn at end of last row. [26 (28, 31, 36, 40) sts]

16 Work even in ldc until 6" from beg of first upper back and shoulder (beg of keyhole).

UPPER BACK EXTENSION

17 Ch 11 (12, 13, 14, 14). Fasten off.

SECOND UPPER BACK

18 With RS facing and working in last full-width row, attach MC2 with sl st in first available st after 2nd marker.

19 **Next Row:** Ch 3 (count as dc), ldc in next and each st across to last 6 (7, 8, 9, 10) sts, turn. [26 (28, 31, 36, 40) sts]

20 **Next Row (Dec Row):** Ch 1 (do not count as st), sk first st, (sc, ch 1) in next st (count as 1 st), ldc in next and each st to end, turn. [25 (27, 30, 35, 39) sts]

Next Row (Dec Row): Ch 3 (count as dc), ldc in next and each st to last 2 sts, dc2tog, turn. [24 (26, 29, 34, 38) sts]

21 Rep step 19 for 2 more times. [20 (22, 25, 30, 34) sts]

22 Work even in ldc until 6" from beg of second upper back (beg of keyhole).

TOP OF KEYHOLE

23 **Next Row (Inc Row):** Ch 3 (count as dc), ldc in next and each st to last st, 2 ldc in last st, turn. [21 (23, 26, 31, 35) sts]

Next Row (Inc Row): Ch 3 (count as dc), ldc in same st (base of ch-3 tch), ldc in next and each st to end, turn. [22 (24, 27, 32, 36) sts]

24 Rep step 23 for 2 more times, do not turn at end of last row. [26 (28, 31, 36, 40) sts]

25 Work even in ldc until 6" from beg of second upper back.

26 Join end of row to end of length of ch on opposite upper back and shoulder for top of keyhole. Fasten off.

27 With RS facing, attach MC2 with sl st in armhole edge of upper back.

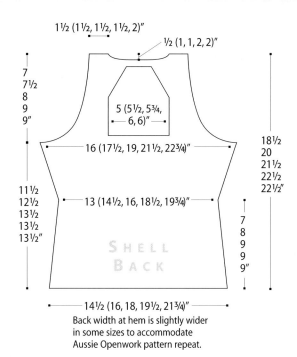

1½ (1½, 1½, 1½, 2)"

½ (1, 1, 2, 2)"

7
7½
8
9
9"

5 (5½, 5¾, 6, 6)"

16 (17½, 19, 21½, 22¾)"

18½
20
21½
22½
22½"

11½
12½
13½
13½
13½"

13 (14½, 16, 18½, 19¾)"

SHELL
BACK

7
8
9
9
9"

14½ (16, 18, 19½, 21¾)"

Back width at hem is slightly wider
in some sizes to accommodate
Aussie Openwork pattern repeat.

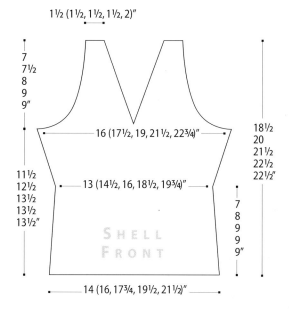

1½ (1½, 1½, 1½, 2)"

7
7½
8
9
9"

16 (17½, 19, 21½, 22¾)"

18½
20
21½
22½
22½"

11½
12½
13½
13½
13½"

13 (14½, 16, 18½, 19¾)"

SHELL
FRONT

7
8
9
9
9"

14 (16, 17¾, 19½, 21½)"

Next Row (Full Back): Ch 1, (do not count as st), sc in first and each st to end, turn.

FIRST SHOULDER

28 **Next Row:** Ch 1 (do not count as st), sc in each of first 3 sts, hdc in each of next 3 sts, ldc in next 3 (3, 4, 4, 7) sts, turn. [9 (9, 10, 10, 13) sts]

EXTRA SMALL ONLY

FASTEN OFF.

SMALL, MEDIUM, LARGE, AND FULL FIGURE ONLY

29 **Next Row:** Ch 3 (count as dc), ldc in next and each st to end, turn. [(9, 10, 10, 13) sts]

30 Rep step 26 once.

SMALL AND MEDIUM ONLY

Fasten off.

LARGE AND FULL FIGURE ONLY

31 Rep step 29 once. Rep step 28 once. Fasten off.

SECOND SHOULDER

32 Join yarn at outer edge. Work as for First Shoulder.

FINISHING

1 If necessary for your yarn, block garment pieces.

2 With RS tog, sew front to back at both shoulders and at both sides.

ARMHOLE EDGING

1 With smaller hk, attach MC2 with sl st at top of side seam.

2 **Rnd 1:** Ch 1, work evenly spaced sc around armhole opening, making sc2tog as necessary for the edge to remain flat, join to beg of rnd with sl st.

3 Attach MC1 with sc to top of side seam.

4 **Rnd 2:** Sc in first and each sc around armhole, join to first st with sl st. Fasten off. Do not turn.

5 Rep edging for rem armhole.

NECK EDGING

1 With smaller hk, attach MC2 with sl st at 1 shoulder.

2 **Rnd 1:** Ch 1, sc in same st, work evenly spaced sc around the neckline, working sc2tog as necessary for the edge to remain flat and working sc3tog at point of V at center front, join to first ch with sl st. Break yarn. Do not turn.

3 **Rnd 2:** Attach MC1, sc in blo of first and every st to end of rnd, working sc3tog at point of V at center front, join to first ch with sl st. Break yarn. Do not turn.

4 **Rnd 3:** Attach MC2, sc in blo of first and every st to end of rnd, working sc2tog at point of V at center front, join to first sc with sl st. Fasten off.

KEYHOLE EDGING

Work as for Neck Edging, but in every row make 3 sc2tog at lower inner corners and 2 sc2tog at upper rounded corners. Fasten off.

SHELL STITCHED BY BARBARA HILLERY, THE FOUNDER, EVENTS COORDINATOR, NEWSLETTER EDITOR, AND PAST PRESIDENT OF THE NEW YORK CITY CROCHET GUILD, INC.

All That Glitters cardigan shown in CGOA Presents *Frolic* and *Sparkle*

L M

ALL THAT GLITTERS

BY MARGRET WILLSON, MEMBER AT LARGE

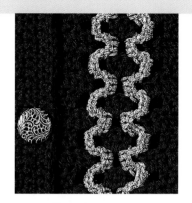

FEATURED STITCHES

Chain (ch); *see page 76*

Chain-space (ch-sp); *see page 80*

Double crochet (dc); *see page 78*

Double crochet 2 stitches together (dc2tog); *see page 80*

Single crochet (sc); *see page 77*

Single crochet 2 stitches together (sc2tog); *see page 80*

Slip stitch (sl st); *see page 77*

GAUGE

21 sts and 11½ rows to 4" in double crochet in MC on F/5 (4 mm) crochet hook, or size required to achieve gauge

TOOLS AND SUPPLIES

E/4 (3.5 mm) crochet hook

F/5 (4 mm) crochet hook, or size required to achieve gauge

Six buttons, ¾" (19 mm) wide

PATTERN POINTERS

Little more than a field of double crochet, the garment pieces feature simple shaping and a modified set-in sleeve for a better fit. A simple filet grid along the front edges and hems offers bars and posts around which to work the surface embellishment.

YARN INFORMATION

Margret chose a firm, medium-weight yarn called CGOA Presents *Sparkle*, in #730 Chrome, for the high-contrast embellishment on this basic black sweater. *Sparkle* is metallized polyester that's knit (cabled) and blended with rayon and nylon. This yields a shiny strand that is flexible enough to stitch, yet firm enough to hold its shape when standing alone on a fabric surface. There's a photo of a single strand in "Yarn Guide" on pages 90–91.

Set the stage to shine with high-impact chrome detailing. The gently curving surface embellishment softens the classic Chanel-inspired silhouette.

	To fit bust	Finished bust†	Shoulder length	Sleeve length	Back length	Lightweight wool (MC)	Medium-weight metallic blend (CC1)
			SIZE			YARN REQUIREMENTS	
EXTRA SMALL	31½"	36½"	3½"	21"	15½"	1,200 yds. (1,097 m)	100 yds. (92 m)
SMALL	34¼"	39½"	4¼"	21"	16"	1,300 yds. (1,189 m)	100 yds. (92 m)
MEDIUM	37¼"	42½"	5"	21"	16"	1,400 yds. (1,280 m)	100 yds. (92 m)
LARGE	41"	45¾"	5¼"	21"	16¾"	1,483 yds. (1,345 m)	100 yds. (92 m)
FULL FIGURE	43¼"	48½"	6"	21"	16¾"	1,556 yds. (1,416 m)	100 yds. (92 m)

†Measurement of buttoned garment

If you would like to stitch in a different yarn, try Plymouth *Gold Rush* (80% viscose, 20% metallized polyester) or Rowan *Lurex Shimmer* (80% viscose, 20% metallized polyester).

The body of the garment is worked in CGOA Presents *Frolic*, in #3 Black. Most yarn shops have a suitable alternative for this medium-twist, classic merino wool. Take a look at Jaeger *Matchmaker 4 Ply* (100% superwash merino wool) and Rowan *4 Ply Soft* (100% merino wool). For more guidance on swapping yarns, see pages 88–89.

The yardage chart at the bottom of page 25 tells you the amount that you need of both yarns. To determine the number of skeins, divide the amount required, as listed in this chart, by the yardage on the wrapper of the skein that you have decided to use.

DOUBLE CROCHET PATTERN

Multiple of any number of sts (add 2 sts for base ch)

Foundation Row: Dc in 4th ch from hk (count as 2 dc), dc in next and each ch to end, turn.

Row 2: Ch 3 (count as dc), dc in next and each dc to end, turn.

Next Rows: Rep row 2.

BACK

1 With F/5 (4 mm) hk, ch 98 (106, 114, 122, 130).

Row 1 (RS): Dc in 4th ch from hk (count as 2 dc), dc in next and each ch to end, turn. [96 (104, 112, 120, 128) sts]

2 Row 2: Ch 3 (count as dc), dc in next and each dc across, turn.

Double Crochet pat established.

3 Work even (rep step 2) until 7¾" from beg.

ARMHOLE SHAPING

4 Next Row (Dec Row): Ch 1 (do not count as st), sl st in first 11 sts, ch 3 (count as dc), dc in next 75 (83, 91, 99, 107) sts, turn. Rem 10 sts unworked.

5 Work even on 76 (84, 92, 100, 108) sts until 6¼ (7, 7, 7¾, 7¾)" from beg of armhole shaping, ending with RS row complete.

LEFT SHOULDER SHAPING

6 Next Row (Dec Row; WS): Ch 3 (count as dc), dc in each of next 17 (21, 25, 28, 31) sts, dc2tog, turn. Rem sts unworked. [19 (23, 27, 30, 33) sts]

7 Next Row: Ch 2 (count as dc), dc in next and each st to end, turn.

8 Next Row (Dec Row): Ch 3 (count as dc), dc in next 17 (21, 25, 27, 31) dc. Rem st unworked. Fasten off. [18 (22, 26, 28, 32) sts]

RIGHT SHOULDER SHAPING

9 With WS facing and working into last full-width row (starting at end of first row of Left Shoulder Shaping), sk 36 (36, 36, 40, 40) sts in center (bottom of neck), attach yarn with sl st in next st.

10 Next Row (Dec Row; WS): Ch 2, dc in next and each st to end, turn. [20 (24, 28, 29, 34) sts]

11 Next Row (Dec Row): Ch 3 (count as dc), dc in next 16 (20, 24, 26, 30) sts, dc2tog, rem tch unworked, turn. [18 (22, 26, 28, 32) sts]

12 Next Row: Ch 3 (count as dc), dc in next and each st to end. Fasten off.

RIGHT FRONT

1 With F/5 (4 mm) hk, ch 48 (52, 56, 60, 64).

Row 1 (RS): Dc in 4th ch from hk (count as 2 dc), dc in next and each ch to end, turn. [46 (50, 54, 58, 62) sts]

2 Row 2: Ch 3 (count as dc), dc in next 5 dc, *ch 1, sk next dc, dc in each of next 3 dc*, rep from * to * 8 (9, 10, 11, 12) more times, dc in each of next 4 sts, turn.

Row 3: Ch 3 (count as dc), dc in each of next 4 sts, *ch 1, sk next dc, dc in next dc, ch 1, sk next ch-sp, dc in next dc*, rep from * to * 8 (9, 10, 11, 12) more times, ch 1, sk next dc, dc in each of next 4 dc, turn.

Row 4: Ch 3 (count as dc), dc in next dc, ch 1, sk next dc, dc in next dc, ch 1, sk next ch-sp, *dc in next dc, dc in next ch-sp, dc in next dc, ch 1, sk next ch-sp*, rep from * to * 8 (9, 10, 11, 12) more times, dc in next dc, ch 1, sk next dc, dc in each of next 3 dc, turn.

Row 5: Ch 3 (count as dc), dc in each of next 2 dc, dc in next ch-sp, dc in next dc, ch 1, sk next ch-sp, *dc in next dc, ch 1, sk next ch-sp*, rep from * to * 8 (9, 10, 11, 12) more times, dc in next dc, dc in next ch-sp, dc in each of next 2 dc, turn.

Row 6: Ch 3 (count as dc), dc in each of next 3 dc, dc in next ch-sp, dc in next dc, *ch 1, sk next ch-sp, dc in next dc, dc in next ch-sp, dc in next dc*, rep from * to * 6 (7, 8, 9, 10) more times, ch 1, sk next ch-sp, dc in next dc, ch 1, sk next ch-sp, dc in next dc, dc in next ch-sp, dc in next dc, ch 1, sk next ch-sp, dc in next dc, ch 1, sk next dc, dc in each of next 3 dc, turn.

Row 7: Ch 3 (count as dc), dc in each of next 2 dc, dc in next ch-sp, dc in next dc, ch 1, sk next ch-sp, dc in next dc, ch 1, sk next dc, dc in next dc, ch 1, sk next ch-sp, dc in each dc and ch-sp to end of row, turn.

Row 8: Ch 3 (count as dc), dc in next 33 (37, 41, 45, 49) dc, ch 1, sk next dc, dc in next dc, ch 1, sk next

ch-sp, dc in next dc, dc in next ch-sp, dc in next dc, ch 1, sk next ch-sp, dc in next dc, ch 1, sk next ch-sp, dc in each of next 3 dc, turn.

Row 9: Ch 3 (count as dc), dc in each of next 2 dc, dc in next ch-sp, dc in next dc, ch 1, sk next ch-sp, dc in next dc, ch 1, sk next dc, dc in next dc, ch 1, sk next ch-sp, dc in next dc, dc in next ch-sp, dc in each dc to end of row, turn.

Rep last 2 rows (steps 8 and 9) for 6 more times.

Row 22: Rep step 8.

ARMHOLE SHAPING

Row 23: As step 9 to last 10 sts, turn. Rem sts unworked. [36 (40, 44, 48, 52) sts]

Row 24: Ch 3 (count as dc), dc in next 23 (27, 31, 35, 39) dc, ch 1, sk next dc, dc in next dc, ch 1, sk ch-sp, dc in next dc, dc in ch-sp, dc in next dc, ch 1, sk ch-sp, dc in next dc, ch 1, sk next dc, dc in each of next 3 dc, turn.

Row 25: Rep step 9 once.

Rep step 13 for 12 (14, 14, 16, 16) more times.

NECK SHAPING

Next Row (Dec Row; WS): Ch 3 (count as dc), dc in next 22 (26, 30, 32, 36) sts, turn. Rem 13 (13, 13, 15, 15) sts unworked. [23 (27, 31, 33, 37) sts]

Next Row (Dec Row): Ch 2 (do not count as st, dec made), dc in next and each st to end, turn. [22 (26, 30, 32, 36) sts]

Next Row (Dec Row): Ch 3 (count as dc), dc across to last 2 sts (do not count ch-2 tch of previous row), dc2tog, turn. [21 (25, 29, 31, 35) sts]

Rep step 16. [20 (24, 28, 30, 34) sts]

Rep step 17. [19 (24, 28, 30, 34) sts]

Next Row (Dec Row): Rep step 16. [18 (22, 26, 28, 32) sts]

Next Row: Ch 3 (count as dc), dc across. Fasten off. [18 (22, 26, 28, 32) sts]

LEFT FRONT

Work as for Right Front to step 2.

Row 2: Ch 3 (count as dc), dc in each of next 6 sts, *ch 1, sk next dc, dc in each of next 3 dc*, rep from * to * 8 (9, 10, 11, 12) more times, dc in each of next 3 dc, turn.

Row 3: Ch 3 (count as dc), dc in each of next 3 dc *ch 1, sk next dc, dc in next dc, ch 1, sk next ch-sp, dc in next dc*, rep from * to * 8 (9, 10, 11, 12) more times, ch 1, sk next dc, dc in each of next 5 dc, turn.

Row 4: Ch 3 (count as dc), dc in each of next 2 dc, ch 1, sk next dc, dc in next dc, *ch 1, sk next ch-sp, dc in next dc, dc in next ch-sp, dc in next dc*, rep from * to * 8 (9, 10, 11, 12) more times, ch 1, sk next ch-sp, dc in next dc, ch 1, sk next dc, dc in each of next 2 dc, turn.

Row 5: Ch 3 (count as dc), dc in next dc, dc in next ch-sp, dc in next dc, *ch 1, sk next ch-sp, dc in next dc, ch 1, sk next dc, dc in next dc*, rep from * to * 8 (9, 10, 11, 12) more times, ch 1, sk next ch-sp, dc in next dc, dc in next ch-sp, dc in each of next 3 dc, turn.

Row 6: Ch 3 (count as dc), dc in each of next 2 dc, ch 1, sk next dc, dc in next dc, ch 1, sk next ch-sp, dc in next dc, dc in next ch-sp, dc in next dc, ch 1, sk next ch-sp, dc in next dc, *ch 1, sk next ch-sp, dc in next dc, dc in next ch-sp, dc in next dc*, rep from * to * 7 (8, 9, 10, 11) more times, dc in each of next 3 dc, turn.

7 **Row 7:** Ch 3 (count as dc), dc in each of next 5 dc, *dc in next ch-sp, dc in each of next 3 dc*, rep from * to * 6 (7, 8, 9, 10) more times, dc in next ch-sp, dc in next dc, ch 1, sk next ch-sp, dc in next dc, ch 1, sk next dc, dc in next dc, ch 1, sk next ch-sp, dc in next dc, dc in next ch-sp, dc in each of next 3 dc, turn.

8 **Row 8:** Ch 3 (count as dc), dc in each of next 2 dc, ch 1, sk next dc, dc in next dc, ch 1, sk next ch-sp, dc in next dc, dc in next ch-sp, dc in next dc, ch 1, sk next ch-sp, dc in next dc, ch 1, sk next dc, dc in next and each dc to end of row, turn.

9 **Row 9:** Ch 3 (count as dc), dc in next and each dc across to first ch-sp, dc in first ch-sp, dc in next dc, ch 1, sk next ch-sp, dc in next dc, ch 1, sk next dc, dc in next dc, ch 1, sk next ch-sp, dc in next dc, dc in next ch-sp, dc in each of next 3 dc, turn.

10 Rep last 2 rows (steps 8 and 9) for 6 more times.

11 Rep step 8.

ARMHOLE SHAPING

12 **Row 23:** Ch 1, sl st in first 11 sts, ch 3 (count as dc), dc in each dc to first ch-sp, dc in first ch-sp, dc in next dc, ch 1, sk next ch-sp, dc in next dc, ch 1, sk next dc, dc in next dc, ch 1, sk next ch-sp, dc in next dc, dc in next ch-sp, dc in each of next 3 dc, turn.

13 **Next Row (Dec Row):** Ch 3 (count as dc), dc in each of next 2 dc, ch 1, sk next dc, dc in next dc, ch 1, sk next ch-sp, dc in next dc, dc in next ch-sp, dc in next dc, ch 1, sk next ch-sp, dc in next dc, ch 1, sk next dc, dc in next and each dc across to ch-3 tch, turn. Rem sl sts unworked. [36 (40, 44, 48, 52) sts]

14 Rep step 9 once.

15 Rep steps 8 and 9 for 12 (14, 14, 16, 16) more times, turn.

NECK SHAPING

16 **Next Row:** Ch 1 (do not count as st), sl st in each of next 14 (14, 14, 16, 16) sts, ch 3 (count as dc), dc in next and each st to end of row, turn.

17 **Next Row (Dec Row):** Ch 3 (count as dc), dc in each st across to last dc and ch-3 tch, dc2tog, turn. Rem sl sts unworked. [22 (26, 30, 32, 36) sts]

18 **Next Row (Dec Row):** Ch 2 (do not count as st), dc in next and each st to end, turn. [21 (25, 29, 31, 35) sts]

19 **Next Row (Dec Row):** Ch 3 (count as dc), dc in next and each st across to last 2 sts, dc2tog, turn. [20 (24, 28, 30, 34) sts]

20 Rep step 18 once. [19 (23, 27, 29, 33) sts]

21 Rep step 19 once. [18 (22, 26, 28, 32) sts]

22 **Next Row (Dec Row):** Ch 2 (do not count as st), dc in next and each st to end. Fasten off. [18 (22, 26, 28, 32) sts]

SLEEVE *(Make 2)*

1 With F/5 (4 mm) hk, ch 49 (49, 53, 53, 57).

Row 1: Dc in 4th ch from hk (count as 2 dc), dc in next and each ch to end, turn. [47 (47, 51, 51, 55) sts]

2 **Row 2:** Ch 3 (count as dc), dc in each of next 4 dc, *ch 1, sk next dc, dc in each of next 3 dc*, rep from * to * 9 (9, 10, 10, 11) more times, dc in each of next 2 dc, turn.

3 **Row 3:** Ch 3 (count as dc), dc in each of next 2 dc, *ch 1, sk next dc, dc in next dc, ch 1, sk next ch-sp, dc in next dc*, rep from * to * 9 (9, 10, 10, 11) more times, ch 1, sk next dc, dc in each of next 3 dc, turn.

4 **Row 4:** Ch 4 (count as dc and ch 1), sk next dc, dc in next dc *ch 1, sk ch-sp, dc in next dc, dc in next ch-sp, dc in next dc*, rep from * to * 9 (9, 10, 10, 11) more times, ch 1, sk next ch-sp, dc in next dc, ch 1, sk next dc, dc in last dc, turn.

5 **Row 5:** Ch 3 (count as dc), dc in ch-sp, dc in next dc, *ch 1, sk next ch-sp, dc in next dc, ch 1, sk next dc, dc in next dc*, rep from * to * 9 (9, 10, 10, 11) more times, ch 1, sk next ch-sp, dc in next dc, dc in next ch-sp, dc in 3rd ch of ch-4 tch, turn.

6 **Row 6:** Ch 3, dc in each of next 2 dc, dc in ch-sp, dc in next dc, *ch 1, sk next ch-sp, dc in next dc, dc in next ch-sp, dc in next dc*, rep from * to * 9 (9, 10, 10, 11) more times, dc in each of next 2 dc, turn.

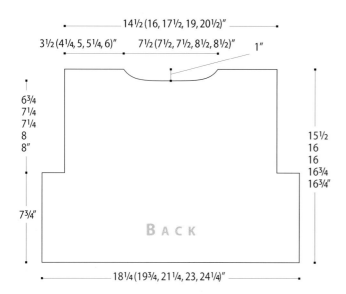

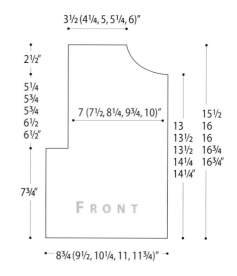

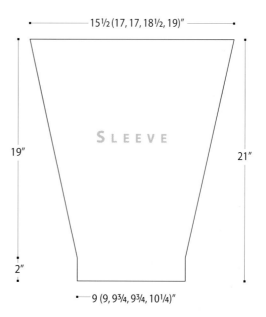

7 **Row 7 (Inc Row):** Ch 3 (count as dc), dc in same st (base of tch), dc in next and each st to end, dc in last st again, turn. [49 (49, 53, 53, 57) sts]

8 **Row 8:** Ch 3 (count as dc), dc in next and each st to end, turn.

9 Rep steps 7 and 8 (last 2 rows) 9 (17, 13, 21, 19) more times. [67 (83, 79, 95, 95) sts]

10 Rep step 7 once. [69 (85, 81, 97, 97) sts]

Work even for 3 rows in dc.

11 Rep step 10 for 6 (2, 4, 0, 1) more times. [81 (89, 89, 97, 99) sts]

12 Work even in dc until 21" from beg. Fasten off.

EMBELLISHMENT

1 With F/5 (4 mm) hk and using the chart on page 30 as a placement guide, you will work around the dc posts and ch-sp bars in filet grid of body hem and fronts and sleeve cuffs.

2 Join Chrome *Sparkle* with sc around dc post (not upper loops) nearest seam line (side seam or underarm seam), 2 sc around same dc, 2 sc around next ch-sp, 3 sc around next dc, cont stitching around posts and ch-sp as shown on Embellishment Charts on page 30 until back at beg, sl st in beg sc. Fasten off.

FINISHING

1 If necessary for your yarn, block garment pieces.

2 With RS tog, sew front to back at both shoulders.

3 Fold a sleeve in half vertically. Place marker at fold on upper edge. Spread joined front and back on table, RS up. Place sleeve

RIGHT FRONT
(Reverse for left front.)

SLEEVE

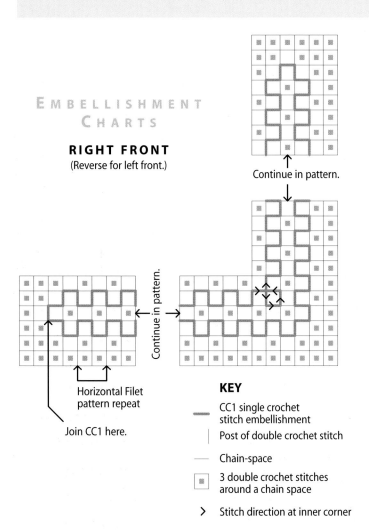

Continue in pattern.

Horizontal Filet
pattern repeat

Join CC1 here.

KEY

— CC1 single crochet
stitch embellishment

| Post of double crochet stitch

— Chain-space

▦ 3 double crochet stitches
around a chain space

⟩ Stitch direction at inner corner

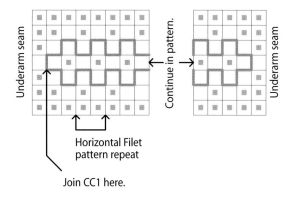

Underarm seam

Continue in pattern.

Underarm seam

Horizontal Filet
pattern repeat

Join CC1 here.

on top, matching stitch marker on upper edge to shoulder. Also match last 5 rows of sleeves to 10 edge sts at underarm. Sew sleeve to body. Join rem sleeve to body in same manner.

4 Refold body and joined sleeves. Join front and back by sewing side and underarm seam. Start at left side seam, sew from hem to armhole, pivot and cont seam to bottom of sleeve. Sew rem side and sleeve seam in same manner.

BUTTONHOLES AND BORDER

1 With RS facing and using smaller hk, join MC with sc at bottom edge of right front.

2 **Row 1:** Work 2 sc in end of each row to beg of neck shaping [74 (78, 78, 82, 82) sc], 3 sc in front neck corner, sc evenly around neck edge, 3 sc in left front neck corner, 2 sc around each row to bottom edge of left front, turn.

3 **Row 2:** Ch 1, sc in each sc, placing 3 sc in center sc at front neck corners, turn.

4 **Buttonholes:** Ch 1 (do not count as st), 2 (2, 2, 4, 4) sc, [ch 3, sk 3, 11 (12, 12, 12, 12) sc] 5 times, ch 3, sk 3, 2 (1, 1, 3, 3) sc, 3 sc in corner, 13 (13, 13, 15, 15) sc, sc2tog twice, sc in each sc around neck edge, sc to within 2 sts of left inside corner, sc2tog twice, 13 (13, 13, 15, 15) sc, 3 sc in front neck corner, sc in each sc to bottom left edge, turn.

5 **Next Row:** Ch 1, sc in each sc and ch, placing 3 sc in each outside corner and 2 sc2tog at each inside corner, turn.

6 **Next Row:** Ch 1, sc in each sc, working 3 sc in each outside corner and 2 sc2tog at each inside corner. Fasten off.

7 Sew buttons to left front.

STRAWBERRY PASSION

By Marinka Kodre-Taylor, member of the
Toronto Hookups in Ontario, Canada

FEATURED STITCHES

Chain (ch); *see page 76*

Double crochet (dc); *see page 78*

Double crochet 2 stitches together
(dc2tog); *see page 80*

Front post double crochet (FPDC);
see page 81

Popcorn; *see page 82*

Shell; *see page 83*

Single crochet (sc); *see page 77*

Slip stitch (sl st); *see page 77*

Treble crochet (tr); *see page 78*

GAUGE

23 stitches and 16 rows to 4" in FPDC
Seed Stitch

TOOLS AND SUPPLIES

F/5 (4 mm) crochet hook, or size
required to achieve gauge

PATTERN POINTERS

This overblouse is reversible, so the
front and back are called "Side 1" and
"Side 2." The stitch pattern is a 1-row
repeat. The finished crocheted fabric
has horizontal ridges, which are
formed by alternating double crochet
and front post double crochet across
a row and then, on the next row,
stacking double crochet on front
post double crochet and front post
double crochet on double crochet.
The ridges are a useful way to count
rows because 1 ridge represents 2
completed rows. On shaping rows,
make a double crochet, rather than a
front post double crochet, in the last
stitch. If working with CGOA Presents
Blithe, use a sharp tapestry needle
when weaving in the ends so that
you can split the yarn.

YARN INFORMATION

The overblouse shown in the photo on
page 32 is worked in CGOA Presents
Blithe #3 Red. This yarn is a medium-
twist blend of cotton, rayon, and nylon
(see pages 90–91 for additional yarn

Pretty maids all in a row won't attract as much attention as this overblouse. Accentuated with a flirty cockleshell edging, this sweater is perfect over a camisole and jeans or a little black dress.

	SIZE				YARN REQUIREMENTS
	To fit bust	Finished bust	Shoulder-and-sleeve length	Back length	Lightweight (such as size 5 cotton) cotton-rayon-nylon
EXTRA SMALL	31½"	37½"	8¾"	18"	1,800 yds. (1,638 m)
SMALL	34¼"	40"	9¼"	18"	1,900 yds. (1,729 m)
MEDIUM	37¼"	42½"	9½"	19"	2,000 yds. (1,820 m)
LARGE	41"	46½"	10½"	19"	2,100 yds. (1,911 m)
FULL FIGURE	43¼"	49½"	11"	20"	2,200 yds. (2,002 m)

Strawberry Passion overblouse shown in CGOA Presents *Blithe*.

L

FPDC SEED STITCH PATTERN

Multiple of 2 sts (add 2 sts for base ch)

Foundation Row: Dc in 4th ch from hk (count as 2 dc), dc in next and each ch to end, turn.

Row 2: Ch 3 (count as dc), *FPDC in next st, dc in next st*, rep from * to * to last st, dc in last st, turn.

Row 3: Ch 3 (count as dc), *FPDC in next dc, dc in next FPDC*, rep from * to * to last st, dc in last st, turn.

Next Rows: Rep row 3.

SIDE 1 *(V Neck)*

1 Ch 110 (118, 124, 136, 144) sts loosely.

Foundation Row (RS): Dc in 4th ch from hk and in each ch to end, turn. [108 (116, 122, 134, 142) sts]

2 **Row 2:** Ch 3 (count as dc), *FPDC in next st, dc in next st*, rep from * to * to last st, dc in last st, turn.

3 **Row 3:** Ch 3 (count as dc), *FPDC in next dc, dc in next FPDC*, rep from * to * to last st, dc in last st, turn.

FPDC Seed Stitch pat established.

4 Work even in pat as established (rep step 3) until 9 (9, 10, 10, 10½)" from beg, ending with WS row complete, turn.

information). Marinka selected her stitches to complement the yarn's qualities. If you would like to use a different yarn, test its personality by making a swatch in the featured stitch. The crocheted fabric needs to drape well and be light enough that it doesn't stretch the sweater out of shape. A suitable yarn will also highlight the stitch and have a slight sheen. Pages 88–89 offer guidance on swapping yarns. Suitable replacement yarns

for this sweater are Skacel *Merino Lace* (100% merino wool) worked as a double strand and Crystal Palace *Baby Georgia* (100% merino wool).

The yardage chart at the bottom of page 31 tells you the amount of yarn that you need. To determine the number of balls, divide the amount required, as listed in this chart, by the yardage on the wrapper of the ball or skein that you have decided to use.

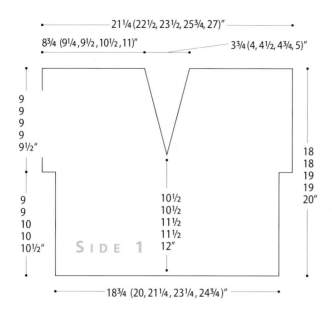

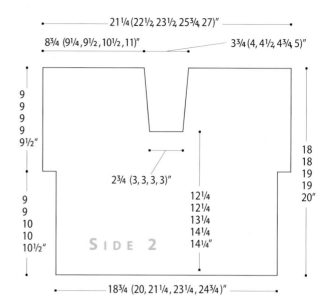

SLEEVE SHAPING

5 **Next Row (Inc Row; RS):** Ch 4 (count as tr), tr in same st as base of tch, 2 tr in each of the next 3 dc, work in pat as established (FPDC into dc, dc into FPDC in previous row) to last 4 dc, 2 tr in each dc to end, turn. [116 (124,130,142,150) sts]

Next Row: Rep row 3 of FPDC Seed Stitch pat.

6 Rep step 5 once more. [124 (132, 138, 150, 158) sts]

7 Work even in pat as established until 10½ (10½, 11½, 11½, 12)" from beg, ending with WS row complete, turn.

RIGHT SHOULDER SHAPING

8 **Next Row (Dec Row; RS):** Work in pat as established across 58 (62, 65, 71, 75) sts, dc2tog, dc in next st (neck edge), turn. Rem sts unworked. [60 (64, 67, 73, 77) sts]

Next Row: Work even in pat as established to end, turn.

9 **Next Row (Dec Row):** Work in pat as established to last 3 sts, dc2tog, dc in last st, turn. [59 (63, 66, 72, 76) sts]

Next Row: Work even in pat as established to end, turn.

10 Rep step 9 for 9 (10, 11, 12, 13) more times. [50 (53, 55, 60, 63) sts]

11 Work even in FPDC Seed Stitch pat until 18 (18, 19, 19, 20)" from beg. Fasten off.

LEFT SHOULDER SHAPING

12 With RS facing and working into last full-width row (starting at end of first row of Side 1 Right Shoulder Shaping), sk 2 sts, attach yarn in next st.

13 **Next Row:** Ch 3 (count as dc), dc2tog, work in pat as established to end, turn. [60 (64, 67, 73, 77) sts]

14 **Next Row:** Work even in pat to end, turn.

15 **Next Row (Dec Row):** Ch 3 (count as dc), dc2tog, work in pat as established to end, turn. [59 (63, 66, 72, 76) sts]

Next Row: Work even in pat as established to end, turn.

16 Rep step 15 for 9 (10, 11, 12, 13) more times. [50 (53, 55, 60, 63) sts]

17 Work even in pat until 18 (18, 19, 19, 20)" from beg. Fasten off.

SIDE 2 *(Modified Square)*

1 Work as for Side 1 to step 8 (Right Shoulder Shaping). Cont working even in pat as established until 12¼ (12¼, 13¼, 14¼, 14¼)" from beg, ending with WS row complete, turn.

LEFT SHOULDER SHAPING

2 **Next Row (Dec Row; RS):** Work in pat as established across 51 (54, 57, 63, 67) sts, dc2tog (dec made near neck edge), dc in last st, turn. Rem sts unworked. [53 (56, 59, 65, 69) sts]

3 Work even in pat as established for 3 rows.

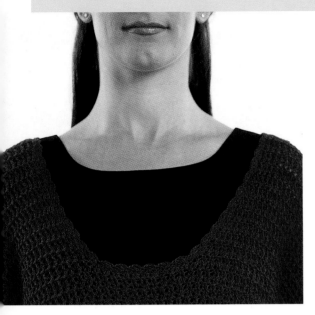

4 Next Row (Dec Row; RS): Work in pat as established to last 3 sts, dc2tog, dc into last st, turn. [52 (55, 58, 64, 68) sts]

5 Work 4 rows even in pat as established, turn.

6 Rep step 4 once. [51 (54, 57, 63, 67) sts]

Next Row: Ch 3 (count as dc), cont in pat as established to end, turn.

7 Rep step 6 for 1 (1, 2, 3, 4) more times. [50 (53, 55, 60, 63) sts]

8 Work even in pat until 18 (18, 19, 19, 20)" from beg. Fasten off.

RIGHT SHOULDER SHAPING

9 With RS facing and working into last full-width row (starting at end of first row of Side 2 Left Shoulder Shaping), sk 16 (18, 18, 18, 18) sts from inner edge of right shoulder, attach yarn in next st.

Next Row (Dec Row): Ch 3 (count as dc), dc2tog, work to end in pat as established, turn. [53 (56, 59, 65, 69) sts]

10 Work even in pat as established for 3 rows, turn.

11 Next Row (Dec Row): Ch 3 (count as dc), dc2tog (dec made near neck edge), work in pat as established to end, turn. [52 (55, 58, 64, 68) sts]

Work even in pat as established for 4 rows.

12 Rep step 11 once. [51 (54, 57, 63, 67) sts]

Next Row: Ch 3 (count as dc), cont in pat as established to end, turn.

13 Rep step 12 for 1 (1, 2, 3, 4) more times. [50 (53, 55, 60, 63) sts]

14 Work even in pat as established until 18 (18, 19, 19, 20)" from beg. Fasten off.

FINISHING

1 If necessary for your yarn, block the sweater pieces.

2 With RS tog, sew front to back at shoulders and sides.

SLEEVE EDGING

1 With RS facing, attach yarn with sl st in a sleeve edge at underarm seam.

Rnd 1: Ch 1, sc in same st, work evenly spaced sc around edge, join to beg of rnd with sl st in first sc. Do not turn. (Near end of rnd, count sts to make sure they're a multiple of 3. If not, adjust rem sts to compensate.)

2 Rnd 2: Ch 4 (count as tr), 6 tr in same st as base of tch, sl st to join top of tch with 6th tr (popcorn made, see page 82), ch 3, *sk next 2 sts, 7 tr in next st, sl st to join first and last tr in group, ch 3*, rep from * to * to last 2 sts, sk 2 sts, join to beg of rnd with sl st in 4th ch of tch. Fasten off.

3 Rep edging for rem sleeve.

HEM EDGING

1 With RS facing, attach yarn with sl st in side seam.

2 Work as for Sleeve Edging, step 2 (rnd 2).

NECK EDGING

1 With RS facing, attach yarn at shoulder.

Rnd 1: Ch 1 (do not count as st), work evenly spaced sc in end of rows (and top of rows when necessary) around front and back neck opening, making sure number of sts is divisible by 3 at end of rnd, join to first ch with sl st. Make sure edge lies flat.

2 Rnd 2: Ch 3, 2 dc in first sc, *sk 3 sts, (sc, ch 2, 2 dc) in next st*, rep from * to * to end, join to tch with sl st. Fasten off.

NORTHERN LIGHTS

By Delma Myers, CGOA nomination chair, historian and founding member of the Ididachain Crochet Guild of Alaska

FEATURED STITCHES

Chain (ch); *see page 76*
Double crochet (dc); *see page 78*
Single crochet (sc); *see page 77*
Slip stitch (sl st); *see page 77*
Reverse single crochet (rsc); *see page 83*

GAUGE

20 sts and 16 rows to 4" in Crumpled Griddle pattern

TOOLS AND SUPPLIES

E/4 (3.5 mm) crochet hook, or size required to achieve gauge

PATTERN POINTERS

The turning chain at the beginning of every row in this pattern is built with either 1 or 3 chain stitches. The number depends on whether the next stitch in the new row is tall (a double crochet) or short (a single crochet). When there is shaping at the beginning of the row, the designer may

intentionally use a 1-stitch turning chain even though the next stitch might be a double crochet. The taller turning chain counts as a stitch, whereas the chain-1 turning chain does not.

Unless shaping interferes with the stitch pattern, the edges start with a chain-3 turning chain and end with a double crochet. This gives you an edge that has nice elasticity and is easier to seam.

This top has cap sleeves, which are part of the body.

YARN INFORMATION

Delma stitched her top, shown on page 36, with a smooth, medium-twist, medium-weight blend of cotton and rayon called *Bliss* from CGOA Presents. Because the yarn is hand painted, the colors are as varied as the

Celestial bodies shine in a classic sweater. Hand-painted colors dance across the crocheted fabric, which is worked in a simple 2-stitch pattern that prevents a blotchy effect.

	SIZE				YARN REQUIREMENTS
	To fit bust	Finished bust	Shoulder-and-sleeve length	Back length	Medium-weight cotton-rayon
EXTRA SMALL	31½"	35½"	6"	19½"	870 yds. (792 m)
SMALL	34¼"	39"	6½"	19½"	946 yds. (861 m)
MEDIUM	37¼"	42"	6¾"	20"	1,048 yds. (954 m)
LARGE	41"	45"	7¼"	20¾"	1,155 yds. (1,051 m)
FULL FIGURE	43¼"	48½"	7½"	21"	1,230 yds. (1,119 m)

Northern Lights
sweater
shown in
CGOA Presents
Bliss.

M

northern lights she sees from her Alaskan home. The featured color is #7 Grape Harvest. Many yarns are suitable for this sweater, including Brown Sheep *Cotton Fine* (80% cotton, 20% merino wool) or Plymouth *Italy Baby* (100% Egyptian cotton). Of course, a local yarn shop can offer other alternatives. To help you, pages 88–89 offer guidance on swapping yarns, and pages 90–91 offer additional information about the CGOA Presents yarn that is featured in the photograph at left.

The yardage chart on page 35 tells you the amount of yarn that you need. To determine the number of balls you need, divide the amount required, as listed in this chart, by the yardage on the wrapper of the ball or skein that you have decided to use.

CRUMPLED GRIDDLE PATTERN

Multiple of 2 sts + 1 st (also add 2 sts for base ch)

Foundation Row: Sc in 4th ch from hk (count as dc and sc), *dc in next ch, sc in next ch*, rep from * to * to last st, dc in last st, turn.

Row 2: Ch 3 (count as dc), *sc in next sc, dc in next dc*, rep from * to * to end, turn.

Next Rows: Rep row 2.

BACK

1 Ch 91 (99, 107, 115, 123).

Foundation Row: Sc in 4th ch from hk (count as dc and sc), *dc in next ch, sc in next ch*, rep from * to * to last st, dc in last st, turn. [89 (97, 105, 113, 121) sts]

2 **Row 2 (RS):** Ch 3 (count as dc), *sc in next sc, dc in next dc*, rep from * to * to end, turn. [89 (97, 105, 113, 121) sts]

Crumpled Griddle pat established.

3 Work even in pat as established (rep step 2) until 17¾ (17¾, 18, 18½, 18¾)" from beg. End with WS row complete, turn.

RIGHT SHOULDER AND NECK SHAPING

4 **Next Row (Dec Row; RS):** Ch 3 (count as dc), work in pat as established (starting with sc in next st) across 35 (37, 39, 41, 43) sts, turn. Rem sts unworked.

5 **Next Row (Dec Row):** Ch 1 (do not count as st), sk first sc (dec made at neck), *dc in next dc, sc in next sc*, rep from * to * to last st, dc in last st, turn. [35 (37, 39, 41, 43) sts]

Next Row (Dec Row): Work across in pat to last dc, turn. Rem dc unworked. [34 (36, 38, 40, 42) sts]

6 Rep step 5 twice. [30 (32, 34, 36, 38) sts]

Work even in pat until 19½ (19½, 20, 20¾, 21)" from beg. Fasten off.

LEFT SHOULDER AND NECK SHAPING

7 With RS facing and working into last full-width row (starting at end of first row of right shoulder shaping), sk 17 (21, 25, 29, 33) sts in center (bottom of neck), attach yarn in next sc.

8 **Next Row (Dec Row; RS):** Dc in next dc, *sc in next sc, dc in next dc,* rep from * to * to end, turn. [36 (38, 40, 42, 44) sts]

9 **Next Row (Dec Row):** Ch 3 (count as st), *sc in next sc, dc in next dc*, rep from * to * to last sc (do not work in ch before last sc), turn. Rem ch and sc unworked. [35 (37, 39, 41, 43) sts]

Next Row (Dec Row): Ch 1 (do not count as st), sk first dc, *sc in next sc, dc in next dc,* rep from * to * to end, turn. [34 (36, 38, 40, 42) sts]

10 Rep step 9 twice. [30 (32, 34, 36, 38) sts]

11 Work even in pat as established until same length as right shoulder. Fasten off.

FRONT

1 Ch 91 (99, 107, 115, 123).

Foundation Row: Sc in 4th ch from hk (count as dc and sc), *dc in next ch, sc in next ch*, rep from * to * to last st, dc in last st, turn.

"If you work with a space-dyed yarn like CGOA Presents Bliss, work with two skeins. For the best color distribution, always stitch with a single strand, but change skeins every second row. Carry the unused strand along the edge."

NANCY BROWN, MEMBER OF THE CROCHET GUILD OF PUGET SOUND IN WASHINGTON

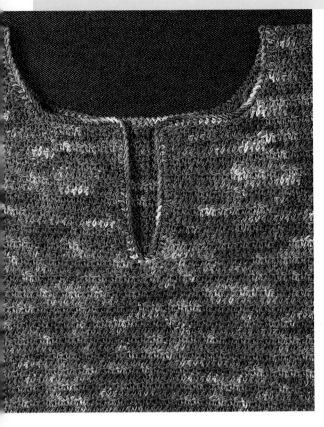

2 **Row 2 (RS):** Ch 3 (count as dc), *sc in next sc, dc in next dc*, rep from * to * to end, turn. [89 (97, 105, 113, 121) sts]

3 Work even in pat as established (rep step 2) until 13 (13, 13, 13½, 13¾)" from beg, ending with WS row complete, turn.

LEFT SHOULDER SHAPING

4 **Next Row (Dec Row; RS):** Ch 3 (count as dc), work in pat as established (starting with sc in next st) across 42 (46, 50, 54, 58) sts, turn. Rem sts unworked.

5 **Next Row:** Ch 3 (count as dc), sc in first sc, *dc in next dc, sc in next sc*, rep from * to * to last st, dc in last st, turn. [43 (47, 51, 55, 59) sts]

6 Cont in pat as established for 14 rows.

NECK SHAPING

7 **Next Row (Dec Row):** Ch 3 (count as dc), work in pat as established across next 35 (37, 39, 41, 43) sts, turn. Rem 7 (9, 11, 13, 15) sts unworked.

8 **Next Row (Dec Row):** Ch 1 (do not count as st), sk first sc, dc in next dc, *sc in next sc, dc in next dc*, rep from * to * to end, turn. [35 (37, 39, 41, 43) sts]

Next Row (Dec Row): Cont in pat as established to last dc, turn. Rem dc and ch unworked. [34 (36, 38, 40, 42) sts]

9 Rep step 8 twice. [30 (32, 34, 36, 38) sts]

10 Work even in pat as established for 3 (3, 5, 6, 6) rows. Fasten off.

RIGHT SHOULDER SHAPING

11 With RS facing and working into last full-width row (starting at end of first row of left shoulder shaping), sk 3 sts (bottom of front slit), attach yarn in next st.

12 **Next Row (Dec Row; RS):** Ch 3 (count as dc), *sc in next sc, dc in next dc*, rep from * to * to end, turn. [43 (47, 51, 55, 59) sts]

13 Work even on short row in pat as established for 15 rows. Fasten off.

NECK SHAPING

14 With RS facing and working on right front shoulder, sk 7 (9, 11, 13, 15) sts (counting from neck of last row worked).

15 **Next Row (Dec Row; RS):** Attach yarn with sc in next st (count as sc), ch 1 (do not count as st), dc in next dc, *sc in next sc, dc in next dc*, rep from * to * to end, turn. [36 (38, 40, 42, 44) sts]

16 **Next Row (Dec Row):** Ch 3 (count as 1 dc), *sc in next sc, dc in next dc*, rep from * to * to last ch and sc, turn. Rem ch and sc unworked. [35 (37, 39, 41, 43) sts]

Next Row (Dec Row): Ch 1 (do not count as st), sk first st, *sc in next sc, dc in next dc*, rep from * to * to end, turn. [34 (36, 38, 40, 42) sts]

17 Rep step 16 twice. [30 (32, 34, 36, 38) sts]

18 Work even in pat for 3 (3, 5, 6, 6) rows or until same length as left shoulder. Fasten off.

FINISHING

1 If necessary for your yarn, block the sweater pieces, *but do not block* Bliss. *This crocheted fabric must be dry-cleaned. Rayon goes limp when washed in water.*

2 With RS tog, sew front to back at both shoulders. Also sew side seams, stopping 7½ (7½, 8, 8½, 8¾)" from shoulder seams.

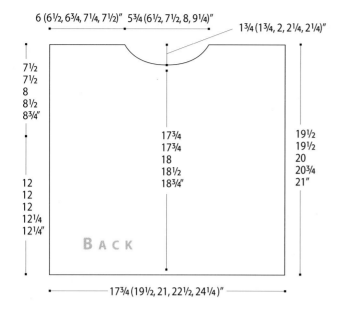

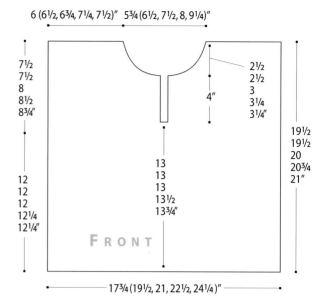

HEM EDGING

1 With RS facing, attach yarn at left side seam at bottom of sweater.

Rnd 1 (RS): Ch 1, sc in each st around, sl st in first ch 1 to join. Do not turn.

2 **Rnd 2:** Ch 1, rsc in each sc around, sl st in first ch 1 to join. Fasten off.

SLEEVE EDGING

1 With RS facing, attach yarn at underarm seam. Work as for Hem Edging. Fasten off.

2 Rep edging for rem sleeve.

NECK EDGING

1 With RS facing, attach yarn at left shoulder seam.

Rnd 1 (Dec Row; RS): Ch 1, work evenly spaced sc around neck, working 3 sc in each outer corner at top of center front slit, [sc in next st, sc2tog (dec made)] at bottom of slit, and sl st in first ch 1 to join. Do not turn.

2 **Rnd 2:** Ch 1, rsc in each st around, sl st in first ch 1 to join. Fasten off.

Short and
Sweet bolero
shown in
CGOA Presents
Celebrity.

F

SHORT AND SWEET

By Joy M. Prescott, member of the
Crochet Guild of Puget Sound in Washington

FEATURED STITCHES

Back post half double crochet
(BPHDC); *see page 79*

Chain (ch); *see page 76*

Front post half double crochet
(FPHDC); *see page 81*

Half double crochet (hdc); *see page 77*

Slip stitch (sl st); *see page 77*

GAUGE

26 sts and 34 rows to 4" in Crunch
Stitch pat

TOOLS AND SUPPLIES

C/2 (3 mm) crochet hook, or size
required to achieve gauge

Stitch marker

PATTERN POINTERS

Joy's bolero is exquisitely shaped, but
this comes at a price: you must pay
careful attention to row and stitch
decreases and increases. In many rows,
you will be working asymmetrical
shaping (increasing or decreasing on
one edge while adjusting a different
number of stitches at the opposite
edge). The border is also unusual. As
you near the upper-front edge, you
need to adjust your thinking because
the border stitch pattern flips so that
the wrong side of the collar becomes
the right side. This way, the correct side
is displayed when the collar is folded
down to its finished position at the
neckline. To start the collar, the border
extends past the front edge so that
you can turn and work back along it.
The border pattern calls for front post
and back post stitches, which can be
difficult to set up in the foundation
row. These instructions include plenty
of guidance to help you through the
rough spots. However, beginning
stitchers should think twice before
tackling this bolero.

Quality is in the details. There's plenty for the well-trained eye to appreciate in this bolero: a wide textured border that follows the edges to become part of the collar, exquisite shaping, and a gently rounded front hem.

	SIZE					YARN REQUIREMENTS
	To fit bust	Finished bust[†]	Shoulder length	Sleeve length	Back length	Fine-weight wool-viscose
EXTRA SMALL	31½"	31½"	4½"	20¾"	16¾"	1,550 yds. (1,411 m)
SMALL	34¼"	35¼"	5¼"	21½"	17"	1,900 yds. (1,729 m)
MEDIUM	37¼"	37½"	5½"	22½"	17"	2,100 yds. (1,911 m)
LARGE	41"	42¼"	6½"	23¼"	17¼"	2,400 yds. (2,184 m)
FULL FIGURE	43¼"	45"	7"	24¼"	17¾"	2,750 yds. (2,503 m)

[†]*Jacket does not meet at center front.*

41

YARN INFORMATION

The Crunch Stitch pattern builds elasticity into crocheted fabric. You can work it with many types of yarn, but the effect is delightful when worked in a tightly twisted yarn like CGOA Presents *Celebrity*. Joy used this, in #9 Periwinkle, to stitch the sweater in the photo on page 40. To examine this fine yarn, see the actual-size photo of a strand on page 90. If you would like to make your bolero in another yarn, the photo in the yarn guide will help you choose a substitute. You might want to consider Crystal Palace *Baby Georgia* (100% mercerized cotton) or Silk City *Wool Crepe Deluxe 80/20*. For more guidance on swapping yarns, see pages 88–89.

The yardage chart at the bottom of page 41 tells you the amount of yarn that you need for your bolero. To determine the number of skeins, divide the amount required, as listed in this chart, by the yardage on the wrapper of the skein that you have decided to use.

CRUNCH STITCH PATTERN

Multiple of 2 sts (add 1 st for base ch)

Foundation Row: Sl st in 3rd ch from hk (count as hdc and sl st), *hdc in next ch, sl st in next ch*, rep from * to * to end, turn.

Row 2: Ch 2 (count as hdc), *sl st in next hdc, hdc in next sl st*, rep from * to * to last st (tch), sl st in top of tch, turn.

Next Rows: Rep row 2.

BACK

1 Ch 115 (127, 135, 149, 157).

   Row 1 (RS): Sl st in 3rd ch from hk (count as hdc and sl st), *hdc in next ch, sl st in next ch*, rep from * to * to end, turn. [114 (126, 134, 148, 156) sts]

2 **Row 2:** Ch 2 (count as hdc), *sl st in next hdc, hdc in next sl st*, rep from * to * to last st (tch), sl st in top of tch, turn.

   Crunch Stitch pat established.

3 Work even in Crunch St pat until 6½ (6½, 6½, 6¾, 7)" from beg, ending with WS row complete.

ARMHOLE SHAPING

4 **Next Row (Dec Beg and End; RS):** Ch 1 (do not count as st), sk first st, sl st in next 4 sts, place marker, ch 2 (count as hdc), *sl st in next hdc, hdc in next sl st*, place marker, rep from * to * to last 5 sts, sl st in next hdc, turn. Rem sts unworked. [106 (118, 126, 140, 148) sts]

5 Rep step 4 once, starting end-of-row dec 5 sts before marker. Rem sts unworked. [98 (110, 118, 132, 140) sts]

6 **Next Row:** Work even in Crunch St pat, turn. Remove marker.

7 **Next Row (Dec Beg and End):** Ch 2 (count as st), sk next 2 sts (hdc and sl st), *sl st in next hdc, hdc in next sl st*, rep from * to * to last 3 sts, sk next hdc and sl st, sl st in top of tch, turn. [94 (106, 114, 128, 136) sts]

8 Rep steps 6 and 7 (last 2 rows) for 2 more times. [86 (98, 106, 120, 128) sts]

9 Work in Crunch St pat for 10 rows, dec at beg and end (rep step 7) on 3rd, 7th, and 10th row. [74 (86, 94, 108, 116) sts]

10 Work even in Crunch St pat until 7¼ (7¼, 7¼, 7¼, 7½)" from beg armhole shaping, ending with WS row complete.

SHOULDER SHAPING

11 **Next Row (Dec Beg and End):** Ch 1, sl st in first 6 sts (do not count as sts, do not work in subsequent rows), hdc in next sl st, *sl st in next hdc, hdc in next sl st*, rep from * to * to last 6 sts, turn. Rem sts unworked. [62 (74, 82, 96, 104) sts]

12 Rep step 11 for 2 more times. [38 (50, 58, 72, 80) sts]

13 **Next Row (Dec Beg and End):** Ch 2 (count as st), sk next 2 sts (hdc and sl st), *sl st in next hdc, hdc in next sl st*, rep from * to * to last 3 sts, sk next hdc and sl st, sl st in top of tch, turn. [34 (46, 54, 68, 76) sts]

14 **Next Row (Dec Beg and End):** Ch 1 (do not count as st), sl st in

first 2 (3, 4, 5, 6) sts (do not count as sts, do not work in subsequent rows), cont across in Crunch St pat as established[†] to last 2 (3, 4, 5, 6) sts, turn. Rem sts unworked. [30 (40, 46, 58, 64) sts]

[†] If next st in previous row is hdc, start with sl st in hdc, ch 2 (count as st) and cont in pat. If next st in previous row is sl st, hdc in sl st and cont in pat.

15 Rep step 14 for 2 (3, 3, 3, 3) more times. [22 (22, 22, 28, 28) sts]

16 Work even in Crunch St pat for 2 rows. Fasten off.

FRONT (Make 2)

1 Ch 23 (29, 33, 41, 45).

Note: For second front, mark row 2 as RS.

Row 1 (RS): Sl st in 3rd ch from hk (count as hdc and sl st), *hdc in next ch, sl st in next ch*, rep from * to * to end, turn. [22 (28, 32, 40, 44) sts]

2 **Row 2:** Ch 2 (count as hdc), *sl st in next hdc, hdc in next sl st*, rep from * to * to last st (tch), sl st in top of tch, turn.

3 **Row 3 (Inc Beg):** Ch 2 (count as hdc), (sl st, hdc) in same st, *sl st in next hdc, hdc in next sl st*, rep from * to * to end, turn. [24 (30, 34, 42, 46) sts]

4 **Row 4 (Inc End):** Ch 2 (count as hdc), *sl st in next hdc, hdc in next sl st*, rep from * to * to last 3 sts, (sl st, hdc, sl st) in next st, hdc in next st, sl st in tch, turn. [26 (32, 36, 44, 48) sts]

5 **Rows 5 and 6:** Rep step 2.

6 Rep steps 3 and 4 (rows 3 and 4) once. [30 (36, 40, 48, 52) sts]

7 Work even in Crunch St pat for 4 rows, turn.

8 **Row 13 (Inc Beg):** Rep step 3. [32 (38, 42, 50, 54) sts]

9 **Row 14:** Rep step 2.

10 **Row 15 (Inc Beg):** Rep step 3. [34 (40, 44, 52, 56) sts]

11 Work even in Crunch St pat for 5 rows, turn.

12 **Row 21 (Inc Beg):** Rep step 3. [36 (42, 46, 54, 58) sts]

13 **Rows 22–24:** Rep step 2.

14 **Row 25 (Inc Beg):** Rep step 3. [38 (44, 48, 56, 60) sts]

15 **Rows 26–31:** Rep step 2.

16 **Row 32 (Inc End):** Rep step 4. [40 (46, 50, 58, 62) sts]

17 Work even in Crunch St pat for 22 (22, 24, 26, 28) rows, inc at end (rep step 4) on 10th (10th, 12th, 14th, 16th) row, on 14th (14th, 16th, 18th, 20th) row, and then on 20th (20th, 22nd, 24th, 26th) row, turn. [46 (52, 56, 64, 68) sts]

ARMHOLE SHAPING

18 **Next Row (Dec End; RS):** Ch 2 (count as hdc), *sl st in next hdc, hdc in next sl st*, rep from * to * to last 3 (5, 7, 9, 11) sts, sl st in next hdc, turn. Rem sts unworked. [44 (48, 50, 56, 58) sts]

19 Rep step 2 once.

20 **Next Row (Dec End; RS):** Ch 2 (count as hdc), *sl st in next hdc, hdc in next sl st*, rep from * to * to last 3 sts, sk next 2 sts, sl st in top of tch, turn. [42 (46, 48, 54, 56) sts]

21 Rep last 2 rows (steps 19 and 20) for 5 more times. [32 (36, 38, 44, 46) sts]

22 Work even in Crunch St pat for 5 rows, turn.

23 **Next Row (Dec End; RS):** Rep step 20. [30 (34, 36, 42, 44) sts]

24 Work even in Crunch St pat once, turn.

25 **Next Row (Dec Beg; RS):** Ch 2 (count as st), sk next 2 sts, *sl st in next hdc, hdc in next sl st*, rep from * to * to last st (tch), sl st in top of tch, turn. [28 (32, 34, 40, 42) sts]

26 Work even in Crunch St pat for 12 rows, turn.

27 **Next Row (Inc End; WS):** Ch 2 (count as hdc), *sl st in next hdc, hdc in next sl st*, rep from * to * to last 3 sts (hdc, sl st, and tch), (sl, hdc, sl) in next hdc, hdc in next sl st, sl st in tch, turn. [30 (34, 36, 42, 44) sts]

28 Work even in Crunch St pat for 30 rows, inc at end (step 27) every 8th, 14th, and 24th row, turn. [36 (40, 42, 48, 50) sts]

SHOULDER SHAPING

29 **Next Row (Dec End; RS):** Ch 2 (count as hdc), *sl st in next hdc, hdc in next sl st*, rep from * to * to last 9 sts, sl st in next hdc, turn. Rem sts unworked. [28 (32, 34, 40, 42) sts]

30 **Next Row (Dec Beg):** Ch 2 (count as st), sk next 2 sts, *sl st in next hdc, hdc in next sl st*, rep from * to last st (tch), sl st in top of tch, turn. [26 (30, 32, 38, 40) sts]

31 **Next Row (Dec End):** Ch 2 (count as hdc), *sl st in next hdc, hdc in next sl st*, rep from * to * 6 (10, 10, 13, 15) more times, sl st in next st, turn. Rem 10 (6, 8, 8, 6) sts unworked. [16 (24, 24, 30, 34) sts]

32 **Next Row (Dec Beg):** Rep step 30. [14 (22, 22, 28, 32) sts]

33 **Next Row (Dec End):** Ch 2 (count as hdc), *sl st in next hdc, hdc in next sl st*, rep from * to * to last 9 sts, sl st in next hdc, turn. [6 (14, 14, 20, 24) sts]

34 **Next Row (Dec Beg, Inc End):** Ch 2 (count as st), sk next 2 sts, *sl st in next hdc, hdc in next sl st*, rep from * to * to last 3 sts, (sl st, hdc, sl st) in next hdc, hdc in next sl st, sl st in tch, turn. [6 (14, 14, 20, 24) sts]

35 **Next Row (Dec End):** Ch 2 (count as hdc), *sl st in next hdc, hdc in next sl st *, rep from * to * for 0 (4, 4, 7, 9) more times, sl st in next hdc, turn. Rem sts unworked. [4 (12, 12, 18, 22) sts]

Extra Small Only: Fasten off.

SMALL, MEDIUM, LARGE, AND FULL FIGURE

36 **Next Row (Dec Beg and End):** Ch 2 (count as st), sk next 2 sts (hdc and sl st), *sl st in next hdc, hdc in next sl st*, rep from * to * for 1(1, 4, 6) more times, sl st in next hdc, turn. Rem sts unworked. [(6, 6, 12, 16) sts]

37 Work even in Crunch St pat for 1 row, turn.

38 **Next Row (Dec Beg):** Ch 2 (count as st), sk next 2 sts, *sl st in next hdc, hdc in next sl st*, rep from * to * 0 (0, 3, 5) more times, sl st in last st, turn. [(4, 4, 10, 14) sts]

39 Work even in Crunch St pat for 1 row. Fasten off.

SLEEVE *(Make 2)*

1 Ch 55 (57, 59, 59, 59).

Row 1 (RS): Sl st in 3rd ch from hk (count as hdc and sl st), *hdc in next ch, sl st in next ch*, rep from * to * to end, turn. [54 (56, 58, 58, 58) sts]

2 **Row 2:** Ch 2 (count as hdc), *sl st in next hdc, hdc in next sl st*, rep from * to * to last st (tch), sl st in top of tch, turn.

3 Work even in Crunch St pat until 4 (3, 2, 1, 1)" from beg, turn. (Larger sizes advance to next step sooner.)

4 **Next Row (Inc Beg and End):** Place marker, ch 2 (count as hdc), (sl st, hdc) in first st (base of tch), *sl st in next hdc, hdc in next sl st*, rep from * to * to last 3 sts, sl st in next st, (hdc, sl st, hdc) in next sl st, sl st in ch-1 tch, turn. [58 (60, 62, 62, 62) sts]

5 Work even in Crunch St pat until 8 (6, 5, 4, 4)" from marker, turn.

6 Rep step 4, moving marker to start of row.

7 Cont working in Crunch St pat, working inc row at the following measurements:
Extra Small: 12"
Small: 9" and 12"
Medium: 8", 11", and 14½"
Large: 6", 8", 10", 12", and 14"
Full Figure: 6", 8", 10", 12", 14", and 16"
[66 (72, 78, 86, 90) sts]

8 Work even in Crunch St pat until 16 (16½, 17, 17½, 18)" from beg, turn.

CAP SHAPING

9 **Next Row (Dec Beg and End):** Ch 2 (count as st), sk first sl st, sl st in each of next 2 sts, ch 2 (count as hdc), *sl st in next hdc, hdc in next sl st*, rep from * to * to last 3 sts, sk next hdc and sl st, sl st in top of tch, turn. [62 (68, 74, 82, 86) sts]

10 Work even in Crunch St pat for 2 rows.

11 **Next Row (Dec Beg and End):** Rep step 9. [58 (64, 70, 78, 82) sts]

12 Rep last 3 rows (steps 10 and 11) until 10 (12, 14, 18, 18) sts rem. Fasten off.

FINISHING

1 If necessary for your yarn, block the sweater pieces.

2 With RS tog, sew fronts to back at shoulders and sides.

3 With RS tog, sew sleeves to joined front and back, placing center of sleeve cap (upper edge) at shoulder seam. Match armhole shaping to sleeve cap shaping.

4 If necessary, press all seams flat.

RIGHT FRONT BORDER

1 Ch 15.

Row 1 (WS): Sl st in 3rd ch from hk (count as hdc and sl st), *hdc in next ch, sl st in next ch*, rep from * to * to end, turn. [14 sts]

2 **Row 2:** Ch 2 (count as hdc), sk first st (base of tch), *sl st in next hdc, FPHDC around next st, sl st in next hdc, hdc in next sl st*, rep from * to * to last st (tch), sl st in top of tch, ch 1, with RS facing, sl st in bottom edge of jacket at center back, ch 1, turn. [14 sts]

3 **Row 3 (WS):** Sk first st, *sl st in next hdc, BPHDC around post st in previous row, sl st in next hdc, hdc in next sl st*, rep from * to * to last st (tch), sl st in top of tch, turn.

4 **Row 4 (RS):** Ch 2 (count as hdc), *sl st in next hdc, FPHDC around next post in previous row, sl st in next hdc, hdc in next sl st*, rep from * to * to end, ch 1, sk 1 st on jacket body, sl st in next st on jacket body, ch 1, turn.

FPHDC pat established.

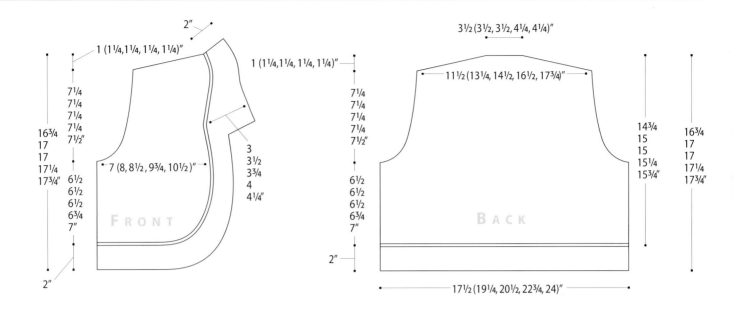

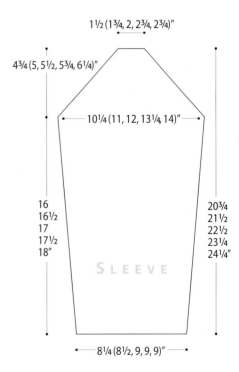

5 Rep last 2 rows (steps 3 and 4) along bolero hem, joining border to curved section of hem without sk 1 st. Once around the curve, cont in pat as established (rep step 4) until 6 (6½, 7, 7½, 8)" from shoulder seam, ending with RS row complete, and join to bolero in established manner. Do not fasten off, do not cut yarn.

COLLAR

6 **Next Row (RS):** Rep step 4, without joining to bolero at end of row.

7 Cont in pat as established until 20 (22, 24, 26, 28) rows are complete, ending with WS row complete.

8 **Next Row (WS):** Pivot to work in edge of rows just completed, ch 2 (count as hdc), sl st in edge st above last joined row, hdc in edge st of next row, rep Crunch St pat as established, working into edge st of each row to inner corner of free portion of border, ending with sl st in edge st of last row, ch 1, sl st in edge st of bolero, ch 1, turn. [20 (22, 24, 26, 28) sts]

9 **Next Row (RS):** Hdc in next sl st, sl st in next hdc, hdc in next sl st, rep Crunch St pat as established until 7 (9, 11, 13, 15) sts worked, *sl st in next hdc, FPHDC around hdc in previous row, sl st in next hdc, hdc in next sl st*, rep from * to * to last st (tch), sl st in top of tch, turn.

10 **Next Row:** Ch 2 (count as hdc), *sl st in next hdc, BPHDC around post st in previous row, sl st in next hdc, hdc in next sl st*, rep from * to *, then work Crunch St pat as established to end of row, ch 1, sk edge st in bolero, sl st in next edge st, ch 1, turn.

11 Cont in FPHDC and Crunch St pats, joining to collar at end of every WS row, until collar reaches center back. Fasten off.

LEFT FRONT BORDER

1 At bottom of bolero back, with RS facing, join yarn to border at center back with sl st in base ch.

Row 1: Working into border base ch, ch 2 (count as hdc), *sl st in next ch, hdc in next ch*, rep from * to * to last ch, sl st in last ch, turn.

2 Cont border and collar, following instructions for Right Front Border and starting at step 2. When left collar meets right collar at center back neckline, fasten off.

3 Sew together ends of right and left collar. Press.

The Big Easy
tunic and cap
shown in
CGOA Presents
Ritz.

M B

THE BIG EASY

BY KATHLEEN STUART, MEMBER OF THE
SOUTH BAY CROCHET CHAPTER IN CALIFORNIA

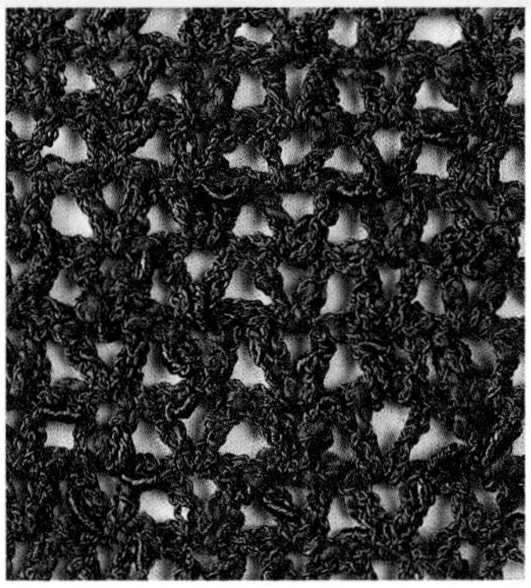

FEATURED STITCHES

Chain (ch); *see page 76*

Chain-space (ch-sp); *see page 80*

Double crochet (dc); *see page 78*

Double crochet 2 stitches together
(dc2tog); *see page 80*

Single crochet (sc); *see page 77*

Slip stitch (sl st); *see page 77*

GAUGE

Tunic: 21 sts (9 V sts) and 10 rows to 4"
in Double Crochet V pattern

Cap: 7 sc and 7 rows to 1½"

TOOLS AND SUPPLIES

G/6 (4.25 mm) crochet hook, or size
required to achieve gauge

Stitch marker (optional)

PATTERN POINTERS

Hate seams? Then you'll enjoy making
this sweater. The bottom of the front
and back are worked separately for
the first few inches. Then the front
and back are joined, creating side slits
at the bottom. The body is worked in
the round as one piece to the start of
the armholes. (Although worked in
the round, you still turn at the end of
every round so that the midsection
will look the same as the rows above
and below.) The sleeves are then created by extending chains from the
body, and the front and back are
again worked separately.

YARN INFORMATION

The yarn used to make The Big Easy is
a richly textured blend of 70% rayon
and 30% cotton, called CGOA
Presents *Ritz*. Here, it's shown in #13
Marine. This yarn is loosely twisted
with thick slubs. A suitable substitute
is Crystal Palace Yarns *Waikiki* (70%
rayon, 30% cotton). Your local yarn
shop may have other great yarns that
will work for this sweater. For more
guidance on swapping yarns, see
pages 88–89.

Celebrate life with a slouchy, extra-long tunic in vibrant blue. It's a breeze to crochet and even more fun to wear with the matching cap. Let the good times roll!

TUNIC	SIZE					YARN REQUIREMENTS
	Note: See page 51 for cap sizes.					*Note: See page 51 for cap yardage.*
	To fit bust	Finished bust	Shoulder length	Sleeve length	Back length	Medium-weight slubbed
EXTRA SMALL	31½"	39½"	6½"	15½"	26"	1,700 yds. (1,547 m)
SMALL	34¼"	43"	7¼"	15¾"	28"	1,800 yds. (1,638 m)
MEDIUM	37¼"	48"	8½"	16"	30½"	1,900 yds. (1,729 m)
LARGE	41"	52"	9½"	16¼"	33"	2,176 yds. (1,980 m)
FULL FIGURE	43¼"	56"	10½"	16¾"	35½"	2,496 yds. (2,272 m)

The yardage chart at the bottom of page 47 tells you the amount of yarn that you need. To determine the number of skeins, divide the amount required, as listed in this chart, by the yardage on the wrapper of the skein that you have decided to use.

DOUBLE CROCHET V PATTERN

Multiple of 3 sts + 1 st (also add 3 sts for base ch)

Foundation Row: Dc in 5th ch from hk (count as 2 dc), ch 1, dc in same ch, *sk 2 ch, (dc, ch 1, dc) in next ch (V st made)*, rep from * to * to last 2 ch, sk 1 ch, dc in last ch, turn.

Row 2: Ch 3 (count as dc), (dc, ch 1, dc) around first and each ch-sp to ch-3 tch, dc in top of tch, turn.

Next Rows: Rep row 2.

BACK HEM

1 Ch 109 (118, 130, 142, 154).

Row 1 (RS): Dc in 5th ch from hk (count as 2 dc), ch 1, dc in same ch, *sk 2 ch, (dc, ch 1, dc) in next ch (V st made)*, rep from * to * to last 2 ch, sk 1 ch, dc in last ch, turn. [35 (38, 42, 46, 50) V sts]

2 **Row 2:** Ch 3, V-st around each ch-sp across, dc in top of ch-3 tch, turn.

Double Crochet V pat established.

3 Rep step 2 (row 2) for 10 more times. Fasten off.

FRONT HEM

1 Work as for back to end of step 3 (12 rows complete). Do not fasten off.

2 **Next Row (Rnd 1):** Ch 3, (dc, ch 1, dc) around each ch-sp across, do not work in last st, do not turn. Cont with Body, below.

BODY

Front: Place back, RS up, beside front (also RS up). Join adjacent edges by working dc2tog in edge stitches (start in last st on front, complete by working in top of edge st of back). Cont with Back, below.

Back: (Dc, ch 1, dc) around first ch-sp, cont in Double Crochet V pat as established to last st, dc in top of last st. Cont with Front, below.

Front: Without twisting pieces, swing front behind back and bring free side edge around to meet free edge of back, thus creating a circle.

Join to beg of rnd with sl st in top of tch at edge of front, turn. [70 (76, 84, 92, 100) V sts.]

3 **Rnd 2:** Ch 3 (count as dc), (dc, ch 1, dc) around each of next 35 (38, 42, 46, 50) ch-sp, sk next dc2tog, (dc, ch 1, dc) around next and each ch-sp to beg of rnd, join to beg of rnd with sl st in top of tch, turn.

4 Work even in rnds (rep rnd 2) until 17½ (19½, 21½, 23½, 25½)" from beg.

UPPER SLEEVES SET-UP

5 Remove hk from working lp.

Right Sleeve: Sk 35 (38, 42, 46, 50) V sts, with length of yarn from another ball, join with sl st between last dc of 35th (38th, 42nd, 46th, 50th) V st and first dc of next V st, ch 85 (85, 88, 88, 91). Fasten off.

6 **Left Sleeve:** Return hk to working lp, ch 87 (87, 90, 90, 93).

UPPER FRONT BODY

7 **Next Row; Left Sleeve:** Dc in 5th ch from hk (count as 2 dc), ch 1, dc in same ch, *sk 2 ch, (dc, ch 1, dc) in next ch*, rep from * to * to last ch, skip last ch. Do not turn. Cont with body. [28 (28, 29, 29, 30) V sts]

Body: (Dc, ch 1, dc) around first ch-sp in body, cont in Double Crochet V pat as established in each of next 35 (38, 42, 46, 50) ch-sp. Cont with Right Sleeve.

Right Sleeve: Working across base ch, sk first ch, *(dc, ch 1, dc) in next ch, sk 2 ch*, rep from * to * to last 2 ch, sk 1 ch, dc in last ch, turn. [91 (94, 100, 104, 110) V sts.]

8 **Next Row:** Ch 3 (count as dc), (dc, ch 1, dc) around each ch-sp to ch-3 tch, dc in top of tch, turn.

9 Rep step 8 until 5½ (5½, 6, 6½, 7)" from beg of sleeve, ending with WS row complete, turn.

LEFT SHOULDER AND SLEEVE SHAPING

10 **Next Row (Dec Row):** Ch 3 (count as dc), *(dc, ch 1, dc) around next 40 (43, 45, 47, 50) ch-sp, dc in next dc (first dc of next V st), turn. Rem sts unworked.

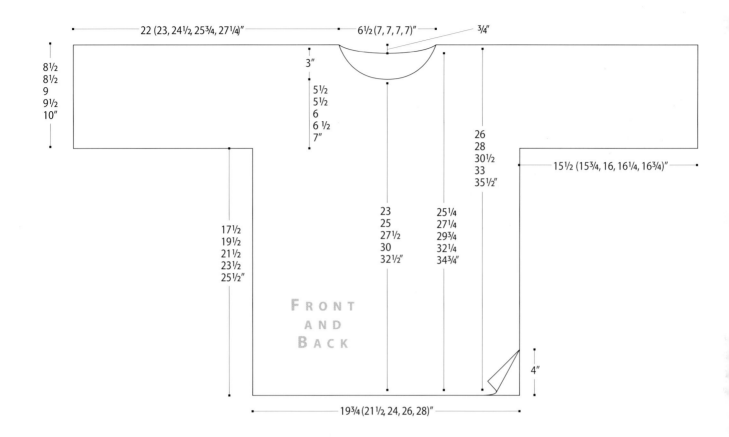

Diagram measurements:

- Top left width: 22 (23, 24½, 25¾, 27¼)"
- Neck: 6½ (7, 7, 7, 7)"
- 3/4"
- Left side heights: 8½ / 8½ / 9 / 9½ / 10"
- 3"
- 5½ / 5½ / 6 / 6½ / 7"
- 26 / 28 / 30½ / 33 / 35½"
- Right side width: 15½ (15¾, 16, 16¼, 16¾)"
- Left lower heights: 17½ / 19½ / 21½ / 23½ / 25½"
- 23 / 25 / 27½ / 30 / 32½"
- 25¼ / 27¼ / 29¾ / 32¼ / 34¾"
- FRONT AND BACK
- 4"
- Bottom width: 19¾ (21½, 24, 26, 28)"

11 **Next Row (Dec Row):** Ch 4 (count as 1 st), sk first dc (under tch), sk first ch-sp, sk next dc (first dc of first V st), dc in next dc, (dc, ch 1, dc) around each ch-sp to end, dc in top of ch-3 tch, turn. [39 (42, 44, 46, 49) V sts]

12 **Next Row:** Ch 3 (count as dc), (dc, ch 1, dc) around each ch-sp across to last dc and ch-4 tch, dc2tog, turn. [39 (42, 44, 46, 49) V sts]

13 **Next Row:** Ch 3, (dc, ch 1, dc) around each ch-sp across to tch, dc in top of ch-3 tch, turn.

14 Rep step 13 for 3 more times. Fasten off.

RIGHT SHOULDER AND SLEEVE SHAPING

15 With RS facing and working into last full-width row (starting at end of first row of Left Shoulder and Sleeve Shaping), sk next 11 (12, 12, 12, 12) ch-sp (include ch-sp next to dc at inner edge of left shoulder), attach yarn with sl st in last dc of last skipped ch-sp.

16 **Next Row (Dec Row):** Ch 3, (dc, ch 1, dc) around each ch-sp to end of sleeve, turn. [40 (43, 45, 47, 50) V sts]

17 **Next Row (Dec Row):** Ch 3, (dc, ch 1, dc) around each ch-sp across to last ch-sp at end of short row, (2 dc, ch 1, dc, tch rem), dc2tog, starting in first dc of last V st and ending in tch, turn. [39 (42, 44, 46, 49) V sts]

18 **Next Row:** Ch 3 (count as dc), (dc, ch 1, dc) around each ch-sp to end, dc in top of tch, turn.

19 Rep step 18 until same length as left shoulder. Fasten off.

UPPER BACK

20 With RS of lower back facing (WS of front sleeves facing), join yarn with sl st at bottom of right sleeve. Work in base chain of sleeve as follows:

21 **Next Row; Right Sleeve:** Ch 3, *(dc, ch 1, dc) in next ch with V st on opposite side*, rep from * to * to end of sleeve, skip last ch. Do not turn. Cont with Body.

Body: (Dc, ch 1, dc) in each of next 35 (38, 42, 46, 50) ch-sp. Cont with Left Sleeve.

Left Sleeve: Working across base ch of second sleeve, sk first ch, (dc, ch 1, dc) in next ch with V st worked in opposite side*, rep from * to * to end, dc in last ch, turn. [91 (94, 100, 104, 110) V sts]

22 Next Row: Ch 3 (count as dc), (dc, ch 1, dc) around each ch-sp to end, dc in top of tch, turn.

23 Rep step 22 for 18 (18, 19, 20, 21) more times.

RIGHT SHOULDER AND SLEEVE SHAPING

24 Next Row (Dec Row): Ch 3, *(dc, ch 1, dc) around next ch-sp*, rep from * to * 38 (41, 43, 45, 48) more times, ending row with dc in first dc of next V st, turn.

25 Next Row: Ch 3, (dc, ch 1, dc) around each ch-sp to end, dc in top of tch. Fasten off.

LEFT SHOULDER AND SLEEVE SHAPING

26 With RS of back facing and working into last full-width row (starting at end of first row of Right Shoulder and Sleeve Shaping), sk the middle 11 (12, 12, 12, 12) ch-sp (include ch-sp next to dc at inner edge of left shoulder), attach yarn with sl st in last dc of last skipped ch-sp.

27 Complete as for Right Shoulder and Sleeve Shaping, starting at step 24.

FINISHING

1 Turn sweater inside out.

2 With RS tog, sew front to back at both sleeve and shoulders.

CAP

BY WILLENA NANTON, PRESIDENT OF THE NEW YORK CITY CROCHET GUILD, INC.

See page 47 for "Featured Stitches," "Gauge," "Tools and Supplies," and "Yarn Information."

PATTERN POINTERS

For the first 3 rounds, the last stitch isn't joined to the first. Thereafter, a slip stitch joins the beginning and end of every row. To track your rows, place a stitch marker at the beginning of the first row and move it to the beginning of every subsequent row as you stitch.

1 Ch 2.

Rnd 1: 6 sc in 2nd ch from hk, place marker. Do not join to beg of rnd, do not turn. [6 sc]

2 Rnd 2: Ch 1 (do not count as st), 2 sc in first and each sc to end of rnd. Do not join to beg of rnd, do not turn. [12 sc]

3 Rnd 3: Ch 1 (do not count as st), sc in first sc, 2 sc in next sc, *sc in next sc, 2 sc in next sc*, rep from * to * to end. Do not join to beg of rnd, do not turn. [18 sc]

4 Rnd 4: Ch 4 (count as dc and ch 1), dc in first sc, ch 1, *dc in next sc, ch 1*, rep from * to * to end of rnd, sl st in 3rd ch of ch-4 at beg of rnd. [38 sts]

5 Rnd 5: Ch 1 (do not count as st), 3 sc in first ch-sp, sk next dc, 2 sc in next ch-sp, sk next dc, *3 sc in next ch-sp, sk next dc, 2 sc in next ch-sp, sk next dc*, rep from * to * to last ch, sk last ch, sl st in first sc at beg of rnd. [45 sc]

6 **Rnd 6:** Ch 5 (count as ch-sp), sk first 2 sc, sc in next sc, *ch 5, sk 2 sc, sc in next sc*, rep from * to * to last 2 sc, ch 5, sl st in sl st of rnd 5. [16 ch-sp]

7 **Rnd 7:** Ch 3 (count as dc), 6 dc around first ch-5 sp, sc around next ch-5 sp, *7 dc in next ch-5 sp, sc in next ch-5 sp*, rep from * to * to end, sl st in top of ch 3 at beg of rnd. [64 sts]

8 **Rnd 8:** Ch 7 (count as dc and ch-sp), sk 2 dc, sc in next dc, ch 4, sk next 3 dc, *(2 dc, ch 2, 2 dc) in next sc, ch 4, sk 3 dc, sc in next dc, ch 4, sk next 3 dc*, rep from * to * to last sc, (2 dc, ch 2, dc) in last sc, sl st in 3rd ch of ch 7 at beg of rnd. [24 ch-sp]

9 **Rnd 9:** Ch 1 (do not count as st), 4 sc around first ch-4 sp, sk next sc, 4 sc around next ch-4 sp, sk 2 dc, 3 sc in ch-2 sp, sk 2 dc, *4 sc around ch-4 sp, sk next sc, 4 sc around next ch-4 sp, sk 2 dc, 3 sc around next ch-2 sp, sk next 2 dc*, rep from * to * to end, sl st in first sc. [88 sc]

10 **Rnd 10:** Ch 1 (do not count as st), sc in same sc as sl st, sc in each of next 42 sc, 2 sc in next sc, sc in next and each of sc to last sc, 2 sc in last sc, sl st in first sc. [90 sc]

11 **Rnd 11:** Ch 1, sc in same sc as sl st, sc in next and each sc to end of rnd, sl st in first sc. [90 sc]

MEDIUM AND LARGE ONLY

Rnd 12: Ch 1 (do not count as st) , sc in same sc as sl st, sc in each of next 13 sc, 2 sc in next sc, *sc in each of next 14 sc, 2 sc in next sc*, rep from * to * to end, sl st in first sc. [96 sc]

Rnd 13: Ch 1 (do not count as st), sc in same sc as sl st, sc in each of next 14 sc, 2 sc in next sc, *sc in each of next 15 sc, 2 sc in next sc*, rep from * to * to end, sl st in first sc. [102 sc]

LARGE ONLY

Rnd 14: Ch 1 (do not count as st), sc in same sc as sl st, sc in next 15 sc, 2 sc in next sc, *sc in next 16 sc, 2 sc in next sc*, rep from * to * to end, sl st in first sc. [108 sc]

Rnd 15: Ch 1 (do not count as st), sc in same sc as sl st, sc in next 16 sc, 2 sc in next sc, *sc in next 17 sc, 2 sc in next sc*, rep from * to * to end, sl st in first sc. [114 sc]

ALL SIZES

12 **Next Rnd:** Ch 1 (do not count as st), sc in same sc as sl st, sc in next and each sc to end, sl st in first sc. [90 (102, 114) sc]

13 **Next Rnd:** Ch 1 (do not count as st), sc in same sc as sl st, sc in next 12 (14, 16) sc, sc2tog, *sc in next 13 (15, 17) sc, sc2tog*, rep from * to * to end, sl st in first sc. [84 (96, 108) sc]

14 **Next Rnd:** Ch 5 (count as dc and ch-sp), 2 dc in same sc as sl st, sk 2 sc, ch 1, sc in next sc, *sk 2 sc, ch 1, (dc, ch 2, 2 dc) in next sc, sk 2 sts, ch 1, sc in next sc*, rep from * to * to last 2 sc, ch 1, sk last 2 sc, sl st in 3rd ch of ch 5 at beg of rnd. [42 (48, 54) ch-sp]

15 **Next Rnd:** Ch 1 (do not count as st), sc around first ch-sp (last 2 sts of tch in previous row), ch 1, sk 2 dc and ch-1 sp, (dc, ch 2, 2 dc) in next sc, ch 1, *sk next ch-1 sp and dc, sc around next ch-2 sp, sk 2 dc and ch-sp, ch 1, (dc, ch 2, 2 dc) in next sc, ch 1*, rep from * to * to last ch-sp, sk ch-sp, sl st in first sc.

16 **Next Rnd:** Ch 5 (count as dc and ch-sp), 2 dc in same sc as sl st, sk first ch-1 sp and next dc, ch 1, sc in next ch-2 sp, ch 1, *sk next 2 dc and ch-sp, (dc, ch 2, 2 dc) in next sc, sk next ch-1 sp and dc, ch 1, sc in next ch-2 sp, ch 1*, rep from * to * to last 2 dc and ch-2 sp, sk 2 dc and ch-2 sp, sl st in 3rd ch of ch 5 at beg of rnd.

17 Rep steps 15 and 16 for 3 times more.

18 Rep step 15 once.

19 **Next Rnd:** Ch 1, sc in same sc as sl st, sc in next ch-1 sp, sk next dc, 3 sc in next ch-2 sp, *sk 2 dc, sc around next ch-1 sp, sc in next sc, sc around next ch-1 sp, sk next dc, 3 sc in next ch-2 sp*, rep from * to * to last 2 dc and ch-1 sp, sl st in first sc. [84 (96, 108) sc]

20 **Next Rnd:** Ch 1, sc in first and each sc to end of rnd, sl st in first sc.

Remove marker. Fasten off. Weave in loose ends.

CAP	SIZE	YARN REQUIREMENTS
	Head circumference	Medium-weight slubbed
SMALL	18"	150 yds. (137 m)
MEDIUM	20½"	150 yds. (137 m)
LARGE	23"	150 yds. (137 m)

Vertical Illusion
tunic shown in
CGOA Presents
Blithe.

L

VERTICAL ILLUSION

BY JENNY KING, MEMBER AT LARGE

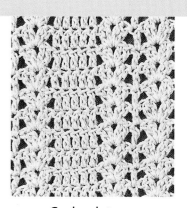

FEATURED STITCHES

Chain (ch); *see page 76*

Chain-space (ch-sp); *see page 80*

Double crochet (dc); *see page 78*

Double crochet in front loop only (dc in flo); *see page 79*

Double crochet two stitches together (dc2tog); *see page 80*

Half double crochet (hdc); *see page 77*

Shell; *see page 83*

Single crochet (sc); *see page 77*

Slip stitch (sl st); *see page 77*

GAUGE

1¾ pat reps† and 12 rows to 4" in Sand and Shells pattern

†1¾ pat reps = shell, dc, shell, 5 dc, shell, dc, shell

TOOLS AND SUPPLIES

B/1 (2.5 mm) crochet hook, or size required to achieve gauge

PATTERN POINTERS

Vertical bands of shells and double crochet posts offer figure-flattering style without taxing your skills. The sizes are set up so that you work complete pattern repeats for the body and switch to double crochet where shaping is necessary. In other words, you don't have to figure out how to decrease while maintaining the Sand and Shells stitch pattern. This is a fun tunic for all skill levels. It's designed to fit without overwhelming the body, diagonal edges eliminate excess fabric at the underarm, and there's a kicky side seam vent for ease of movement.

YARN INFORMATION

Proving yet again that crocheted fabric doesn't have to be stiff, Vertical Illusion drapes beautifully over the

Go back to the shore one more time by slipping into this sophisticated tunic that features a delicate Sand and Shells stitch pattern worked in the natural color of an ocean landscape.

			SIZE			YARN REQUIREMENTS	
	To fit bust	Finished bust	Shoulder length	Sleeve length	Body length	Lightweight (such as size 5 cotton) cotton-rayon-nylon	
EXTRA SMALL	31½"	34½"	4"	15½"	20¼"	1,600 yds. (1,456 m)	
SMALL	34¼"	39"	4¼"	15¾"	22"	1,600 yds. (1,456 m)	
MEDIUM	37¼"	44"	4¼"	16"	23¼"	1,800 yds. (1,638 m)	
LARGE	41"	49"	4½"	16¼"	24¼"	2,200 yds. (2,002 m)	
FULL FIGURE	43¼"	53½"	4½"	17½"	26¾"	2,450 yds. (2,221 m)	

body. A slightly open stitch pattern and the right yarn make all the difference. The sweater shown was stitched in CGOA Presents *Blithe* #19 Bone China, which is a medium-twist blend of cotton, nylon, and rayon. For the best results, work your version in a yarn that has lustrous shine and a soft hand. Suitable replacement yarns for this sweater are Skacel *Merino Lace* (100% merino wool) worked as a double strand and Crystal Palace *Baby Georgia* (100% merino wool). Guidance on swapping yarns is offered on pages 88–89.

The yardage chart at the bottom of page 53 tells you the amount of yarn that you need. To determine the number of skeins, divide the amount required, as listed in this chart, by the yardage on the wrapper of the skein that you have decided to use.

SAND AND SHELLS PATTERN

Multiple of 16 sts + 5 sts (also add 2 sts for base ch)

Foundation Row: Dc in the 4th ch from hk (count as 2 dc), dc in next 3 ch, *sk next 2 ch, (2 dc, ch 1, 2 dc) in next ch (shell made), sk next 2 ch, dc in next ch, sk next 2 ch, shell in next ch, sk 2 ch, dc in next 5 ch*, rep from * to * to end, turn.

Row 2: Ch 3 (count as dc), dc in next 4 dc, *shell in center ch-sp of next shell, dc in next (single) dc, shell in center ch-sp of next shell, dc in flo in each of next 5 dc*, rep from * to * to end, turn.

Next Rows: Rep row 2.

BACK

1 Ch 119 (135, 151, 167, 183).

Row 1 (RS): Dc in 4th ch from hk (count as 2 dc), dc in next 3 ch, *sk next 2 ch, (2 dc, ch 1, 2 dc) in next ch (shell made), sk next 2 ch, dc in next ch, sk next 2 ch, shell in next ch, sk 2 ch, dc in next 5 ch*, rep from * to * to end, turn. [117 (133, 149, 165, 181) sts or 7 (8, 9, 10, 11) Sand and Shells pat reps and 5 dc at beg]

Row 2: Ch 3 (count as dc), dc in next 4 dc, *shell in ch-sp of next shell, dc in next (single) dc, shell in ch-sp of next shell, dc in flo in each of next 5 dc*, rep from * to * to end, turn.

Sand and Shells pat established.

2 Work in Sand and Shells pat until 13 (13¾, 14½, 15, 17)" from beg, turn.

3 **Next Row:** Ch 3 (count as dc), dc in next 15 sts (dc in each dc and dc around each ch-sp), dc in flo in each of next 5 dc, *shell in ch-sp of next shell, dc in next (single) dc, shell in ch-sp of next shell, dc in flo in each of next 5 dc*, rep from * to * 4 (5, 6, 7, 8) more times, dc in next 16 sts to end, turn.

ARMHOLE SHAPING

4 **Next Row (Dec Row):** Ch 1 (do not count as st), sk first dc, (sc, ch 1) in 2nd st (count as 1 st), dc2tog, dc in each of next 17 dc, *shell in ch-sp of next shell, dc in next (single) dc, shell in ch-sp of next shell, dc in flo in each of next 5 dc*, rep from * to * 4 (5, 6, 7, 8) more times, dc in each dc to last 4 sts, dc2tog twice, turn. [113 (129, 145, 161, 177) sts]

5 **Next Row (Dec Row):** Ch 1 (do not count as st), sk first dc, (sc, ch 1) in 2nd st (count as 1 st), dc2tog, cont in pat, working dc in dc and shells in shell ch-sp (sts change to all dc near end of row) to last 4 sts (3 dc and dc2tog in previous row), dc2tog twice, turn. [109 (125, 141, 157, 173) sts]

6 Rep step 5 (last dec row) for 3 more times. [97 (113, 129, 145, 161) sts]

7 Work even in Sand and Shells pat as established until 7 (8, 8½, 9, 9½)" from beg of armhole shaping, turn.

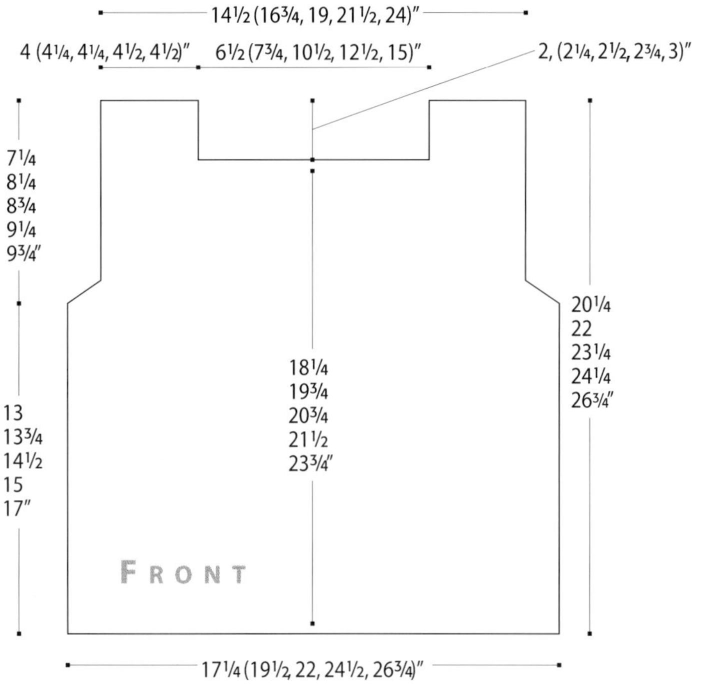
14½ (16¾, 19, 21½, 24)"
4 (4¼, 4¼, 4½, 4½)"
6½ (7¾, 10½, 12½, 15)"
2, (2¼, 2½, 2¾, 3)"
7¼
8¼
8¾
9¼
9¾"
13
13¾
14½
15
17"
18¼
19¾
20¾
21½
23¾"
20¼
22
23¼
24¼
26¾"
FRONT
17¼ (19½, 22, 24½, 26¾)"

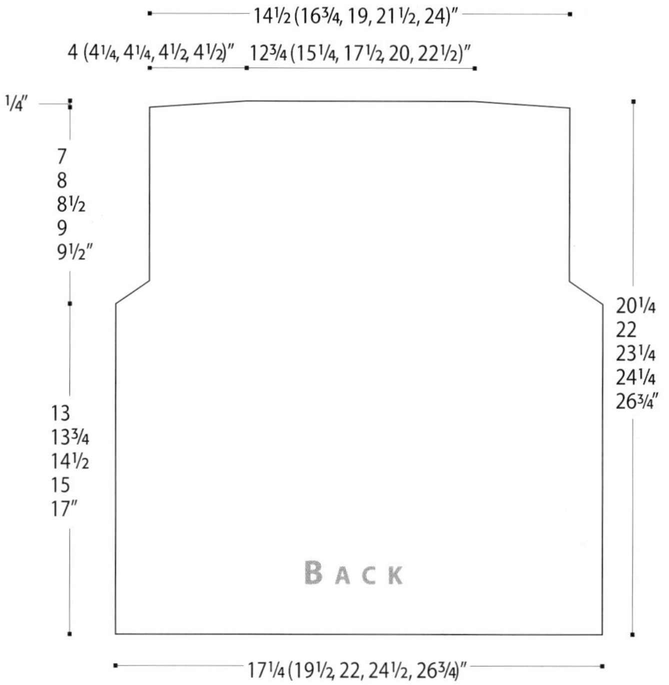
14½ (16¾, 19, 21½, 24)"
4 (4¼, 4¼, 4½, 4½)"
12¾ (15¼, 17½, 20, 22½)"
¼"
7
8
8½
9
9½"
13
13¾
14½
15
17"
20¼
22
23¼
24¼
26¾"
BACK
17¼ (19½, 22, 24½, 26¾)"

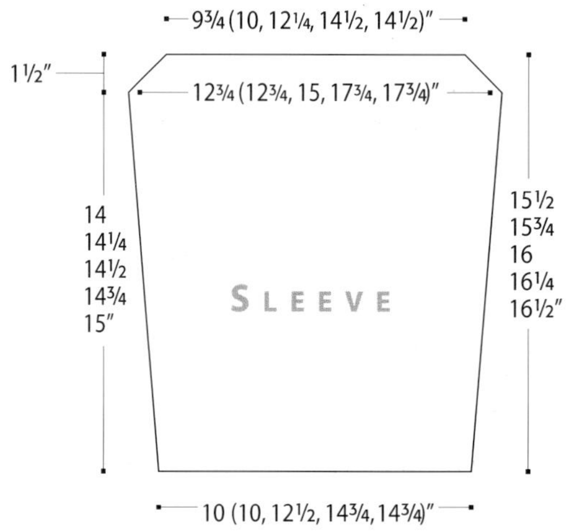
9¾ (10, 12¼, 14½, 14½)"
1½"
12¾ (12¾, 15, 17¾, 17¾)"
14
14¼
14½
14¾
15"
15½
15¾
16
16¼
16½"
SLEEVE
10 (10, 12½, 14¾, 14¾)"

SHOULDER SHAPING

8 **Next Row (Dec Row):** Sl st in first 5 dc, (2 sc, ch 1, 2 sc) in ch-sp of next shell (sc shell made), hdc in next (single) dc, (2 hdc, ch 1, 2 hdc) in ch-sp of next shell (hdc shell made), work across in Sand and Shells pat as established in previous row (using dc sts) to last 2 shells, hdc shell in next shell, hdc in next (single) dc, sc shell in next shell. Rem 5 sts unworked. Fasten off. Note: Sc shell and hdc shell are only used for back shoulder shaping.

FRONT

1 Work as for Back to step 7.

2 Work even in Sand and Shells pat for 18¼ (19¾, 20¾, 21½, 23¾)" from beg, ending with WS row complete, turn.

RIGHT SHOULDER SHAPING

3 **Next Row (RS):** Ch 3, dc in next 4 dc, shell in next shell, dc in next (single) dc, shell in next shell, dc in next 5 dc, shell in next shell, dc in next (single) dc, dc in first 1 (2, 2, 3, 3) sts of next shell, turn. Rem sts unworked. [28 (29, 29, 30, 30) sts]

4 Work even in Sand and Shells pat as established [dc in (single) dc, shell in shell] until 2 (2¼, 2½, 2¾, 3)" from beg of shoulder shaping. Fasten off.

LEFT SHOULDER SHAPING

5 With RS facing and working into last full-width row (starting at end of first row of Right Shoulder Shaping), sk 29 (43, 59, 73, 89) sts (bottom of neck), attach yarn with sl st in next st.

6 **Next Row:** Ch 3 (count as dc), dc in next 0 (1, 1, 2, 2) sts, cont to end of row in pat, working dc in (single) dc and shells in shells, turn. [28 (29, 29, 30, 30) sts]

7 Work even in Sand and Shells pat as established [dc in (single) dc, shell in shell] until same length as right shoulder. Fasten off.

SLEEVE (Make 2)

1 Ch 71 (71, 87, 103, 103).

Row 1: Dc in 4th ch from hk (count as 2 dc), dc in next 3 ch, *sk next 2 ch, (2 dc, ch 1, 2 dc) in next ch (shell made), sk next 2 ch, dc in next ch, *sk next 2 ch, shell in next ch, sk 2 ch, dc in next 5 ch*, rep from * to * to end, turn. [69 (69, 85, 101, 101) sts or 4 (4, 5, 6, 6) shells and 5 dc at beg]

2 Next Row (Inc Row): Ch 3 (count as dc), dc in same st as base of tch, cont across row in pat as established, working dc in (single) dc and shells in shells, turn. [70 (70, 86, 102, 102) sts or 4 (4, 5, 6, 6) Sand and Shells pat reps and 6 dc at beg]

3 Rep step 2 (inc only at beg of row) to 86 (86, 103, 119, 119) sts, turn. Do not work new Sand and Shells pat rep into dc inc along edges. At end of inc, you will still have 4 (4, 5, 6, 6) Sand and Shells pat reps.

Cont in pat as established until 14 (14¼, 14½, 14¾, 15)" from beg.

4 Next Row (Dec Row): Ch 1 (do not count as st), sk first dc, (sc, ch 1) in 2nd st (count as 1 st), dc2tog, cont across in pat as established, working dc in (single) dc and shells in shells, to last 4 sts, dc2tog twice, turn. [82 (82, 99, 115, 115) sts]

5 Rep step 4 (dec row) for 4 more times. Fasten off. [66 (66, 83, 99, 99) sts]

FINISHING

1 If necessary for your yarn, block the sweater pieces.

2 Fold a sleeve in half vertically. Place marker at fold on upper edge. Spread joined front and back on table, RS up. Place sleeve on top, matching stitch marker on upper edge to shoulder seam. Sew sleeve to body.

3 Join rem sleeve to body in same manner.

4 Refold body and joined sleeves. Join front and back by sewing a side and underarm seam. Start at left side seam 3 (3, 3½, 4, 4)" above hem (side slit made), sew from hem to armhole, pivot, and cont seam to bottom of sleeve. Sew rem side and sleeve seam in same manner.

NECK EDGING

1 With RS facing, join yarn at back of neck with sc.

Rnd 1: Work sc evenly spaced around neckline. Do not join to beg of rnd, do not turn.

2 Rnd 2: Sc in flo in first and every st to end of rnd. Do not join, do not turn.

3 Rep step 2. Fasten off.

HEM EDGING

1 With RS facing, join yarn at edge of back hem with sc.

2 Rnd 1: Work sc evenly spaced around hem and edges of side slits, working sc3tog at top of slits and 3 sc in each corner. Do not join to beg of rnd, do not turn.

3 Rep step 2. Fasten off.

CUFF EDGING

1 With RS facing, join yarn at under-arm seam with sc.

2 Rnd 1: Work sc evenly spaced around edge. Do not join to beg of rnd, do not turn.

3 Rep step 2. Fasten off.

4 Rep edging for rem sleeve. Fold over twice for cuffs.

FALLSCAPE

BY MARGRET WILLSON, MEMBER AT LARGE

FEATURED STITCHES

Chain (ch); *see page 76*

Double crochet (dc); *see page 78*

Half double crochet (hdc); *see page 77*

Shell; *see page 83*

Single crochet (sc); *see page 77*

Slip stitch (sl st); *see page 77*

Treble crochet (tr); *see page 78*

GAUGE

4 shells and 5 sc to 4", 14 rows to 4" in Solid Shell pattern

TOOLS AND SUPPLIES

E/4 (3.5 mm) crochet hook, or size required to achieve gauge

PATTERN POINTERS

A lightweight rayon yarn worked in a Solid Shell stitch makes a crocheted fabric with luxurious drape. To enhance the effect, treble crochet stitches are used in place of the usual doubles. But the wonderful character-istics of the yarn and stitch pattern can be challenging during stitching. The fabric is unstable; when held up, the weight of the finished rows will lengthen the stitched piece. It's impor-tant that you measure the length only with the stitched fabric flat and spread to the finished width that is noted on the schematic (see page 60).

The crocheted fabric will adjust to your body shape. The effect is fitted, despite the 5" of ease (additional sweater width beyond what is needed for your body measurements). In fact, when worn, the tunic body and sleeves will be about 3" longer than the measure-ments shown on the schematics.

When worked even, the right-side rows have 1 less shell than the wrong-side rows. A half shell at an edge is included in the end-of-row shell count.

Quiet confidence and elegance carry you through a special event. Merely slip this richly colored top over a basic shift dress. The soft, sensual yarn enhances a humble silhouette.

	SIZE					YARN REQUIREMENTS
	To fit bust	Finished bust	Shoulder length	Sleeve length	Back length	Fine-weight rayon
EXTRA SMALL	31½"	37"	3½"	15½"	21¼"	3,200 yds. (2,912 m)
SMALL	34¼"	38½"	3½"	15½"	22"	3,400 yds. (3,094 m)
MEDIUM	37¼"	42"	4½"	16"	22¾"	3,800 yds. (3,458 m)
LARGE	41"	46"	5½"	16½"	23½"	4,200 yds. (3,822 m)
FULL FIGURE	43¼"	48"	5½"	16½"	25½"	4,600 yds. (4,186 m)

Fallscape tunic shown in CGOA Presents *Splendor.*

L

SOLID SHELL PATTERN

Multiple of 8 sts + 1 st (also add 1 st for base ch)

Foundation Row (RS): Sc in 2nd ch from hk (count as sc), *sk 3 ch, 5 tr in next ch (shell made), sk 3 ch, sc in next ch*, rep from * to * to end of row, turn.

Row 2 (WS): Ch 4 (count as tr), 2 tr in first sc (base of tch), (half shell made), *sc in 3rd tr of next shell, 5 tr in next sc (shell made)*, rep from * to * to last shell and sc, sc in 3rd tr of last shell, 3 tr in last sc, turn.

Row 3: Ch 1 (do not count as st), sc in first tr, *shell in next sc, sc in 3rd tr of next shell*, rep from * to * to last sc and half shell, shell in last sc, sc in top of 4-ch tch, turn.

Next Rows: Rep rows 2 and 3.

BACK

1 Ch 162 (170, 186, 202, 210).

Row 1 (RS): Sc in 2nd ch from hk (count as sc), *sk 3 ch, 5 tr in next ch (shell made), sk 3 ch, sc in next ch*, rep from * to * to end, turn. [20 (21, 23, 25, 26) shells]

2 **Row 2:** Ch 4 (count as tr), 2 tr in first sc (base of tch), (half shell made), *sc in 3rd tr of next shell, 5 tr in next sc (shell made)*, rep from * to * to last shell and sc, sc in 3rd tr of last shell, 3 tr in last sc, turn. [21 (22, 24, 26, 27) shells]

YARN INFORMATION

The key to making Fallscape successfully is the yarn selection. Margret stitched hers with a light-weight rayon called CGOA Presents *Splendor* #5 Brown-Olive. Berroco *Lang Opal* (58% polyamide, 42% viscose) is another great choice. *Splendor* is cabled (see the photo on page 91), but a twisted yarn will work just as well. Your local yarn shop can suggest other yarn choices. In addition, pages 88–89 offer guidance on swapping yarns, and pages 90–91

offer more information about the CGOA Presents yarn that's featured in the photograph. When you find a yarn that you like, make a 6" swatch to verify that the crocheted fabric has a soft, almost slinky drape.

The chart at the bottom of page 57 tells you the amount of yarn that you need. To determine the number of balls you need, divide the amount required, as listed in this chart, by the yardage on the wrapper of the ball or skein that you have decided to use.

Row 3: Ch 1 (do not count as st), sc in first tr, *shell in next sc, sc in 3rd tr of next shell*, rep from * to * to last sc and shell, shell in last sc, sc in top of 4-ch tch, turn. [20 (21, 23, 25, 26) shells]

Solid Shell pat established.

3 Rep step 2 (last 2 rows) until 14¾ (14¾, 15, 15¼, 16¼)" from beg. On WS rows there are 21 (22, 24, 26, 27) shells. On RS rows there are 20 (21, 23, 25, 26) shells. End with RS row complete, turn.

ARMHOLE SHAPING

4 **Next Row (Dec Row; WS):** Ch 1, sk first st, sl st in each of next 2 tr, sc in next tr, *shell in next sc, sc in 3rd tr of next shell*, rep from * to * across, ending with sc in 3rd tr of last complete shell, turn. Rem 3 sts unworked. [19 (20, 22, 24, 25) shells]

5 Rep step 4 for 3 more times. [16 (17, 19, 21, 22) shells]

6 Starting with Solid Shell pat, row 2, work even in pat for 5 (5¾, 6¼, 6¾, 7½)" from beg of armhole shaping. End with RS row complete, turn. [16 (17, 19, 21, 22) shells]

LEFT SHOULDER SHAPING

7 **Next Row (Dec Row; WS):** Ch 4 (count as tr), 2 tr in first sc (base of tch), (half shell made), sc in 3rd tr of next shell, *shell in next sc, sc in 3rd tr of next shell*, rep from * to * 4 (4, 5, 6, 6) more times, turn. Rem sts unworked. [6 (6, 7, 8, 8) shells]

8 **Next Row (Dec Row):** Ch 1 (do not count as st), sk first sc, sl st in each of next 2 tr, sc in next tr, shell in next sc, *sc in 3rd tr of next shell, shell in next sc*, rep from * to * across to half shell at edge, sc in last tr, turn. [5 (5, 6, 7, 7) shells]

9 **Next Row (Dec Row):** Ch 4 (count as tr), 2 tr in first sc (base of tch), sc in 3rd tr of next shell, *shell in next sc, sc in 3rd tr of next shell*, rep from * to * 3 (3, 4, 5, 5) more times, turn. Rem sc unworked.

10 **Next Row (Dec Row):** Rep step 8. [4 (4, 5, 6, 6) shells]

11 **Next Row:** This row fills in the curves to make a straight edge for seaming. Ch 3 (do not count as st), sk first sc, *hdc in first tr of shell, sc in 2nd tr of shell, sl st in 3rd tr of shell, sc in 4th tr of shell, hdc in 5th tr of shell, dc in next sc*, rep from * to * to end. Fasten off.

RIGHT SHOULDER SHAPING

12 With WS facing and working into last full-width row (starting at end of first row of Left Shoulder Shaping), sk 4 (5, 5, 5, 6) complete shells, join with sc in 3rd tr of next shell.

13 **Next Row (Dec Row):** *Shell in next sc, sc in 3rd tr of next shell*, rep from * to * to end, 3 tr in last sc, turn.

14 **Next Row (Dec Row):** Ch 1, sc in first tr, *shell in next sc, sc in 3rd tr of next shell*, rep from * to * 4 (4, 5, 6, 6) more times, turn. Rem shell unworked.

15 **Next Row (Dec Row):** Ch 1, sk first sc, sl st in each of next 2 tr, sc in next tr, shell in next sc, *sc in 3rd tr of next shell, shell in next sc*, rep from * to * to last shell and sc, sc in 3rd tr of shell, 3 tr in last sc, turn. [5 (5, 6, 7, 7) shells]

16 **Next Row (Dec Row):** Ch 1, sc in first tr, *shell in next sc, sc in 3rd tr of next shell*, rep from * to * 3 (3, 4, 5, 5) more times, turn.

17 **Next Row (Dec Row):** Ch 3 (do not count as st), sk first sc, *hdc in first tr of shell, sc in 2nd tr of shell, sl st in 3rd tr of shell, sc in 4th tr of shell, hdc in 5th tr of shell, dc in next sc*, rep from * to * to end. Fasten off.

FRONT

Work as for Back.

SLEEVE *(Make 2)*

1 Ch 138 (146, 154, 162, 170).

Row 1: Sc in 2nd ch from hk (count as sc), *sk 3 ch, shell in next ch, sk 3 ch, sc in next ch*, rep from * to * to end, turn. [17 (18, 19, 20, 21) shells]

2 **Row 2:** Ch 4 (count as tr), 2 tr in first sc, *sc in 3rd tr of next shell, shell in next sc*, rep from * to * to last shell and sc, sc in 3rd tr of last shell, 3 tr in last sc, turn.

Row 3: Ch 1 (do not count as st), sc in first tr, *shell in next sc, sc in 3rd tr of next shell*, rep from * to * to last sc and shell, shell in last sc, sc in top of 4-ch tch, turn.

3 Work even in Solid Shell pat (rep step 2) until 14 (14, 14½, 15, 15)" from beg, ending with RS row complete, turn.

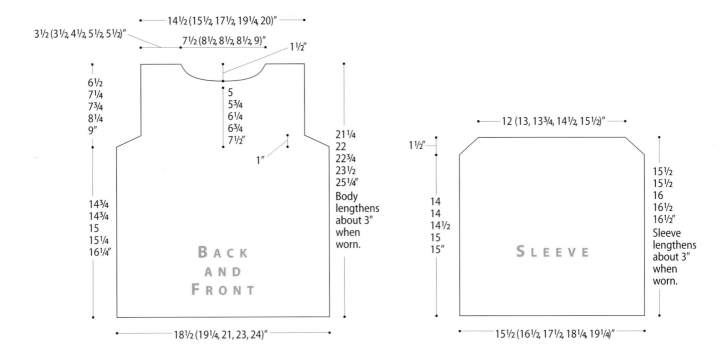

4 Next Row (Dec Row; WS): Ch 1, sk first st, sl st in each of next 2 tr, sc in next tr, *shell in next sc, sc in 3rd tr of next shell*, rep from * to *, ending with sc in 3rd tr of last complete shell, turn. Rem 3 sts unworked. [16 (17, 18, 19, 20) shells]

5 Rep step 4 (last row) for 3 more times. [13 (14, 15, 16, 17) shells]

6 Next Row: Ch 3, sk first sc, *hdc in first tr of shell, sc in 2nd tr of shell, sl st in 3rd tr of shell, sc in 4th tr of shell, hdc in 5th tr of shell, dc in next sc*, rep from * to * to end of row. Fasten off.

FINISHING

1 If necessary for your yarn, block the sweater pieces. Do not block crocheted pieces made with rayon yarn. Moisture flattens and softens rayon and may also cause shrinkage. Check the care information on the yarn wrapper.

2 With RS tog, sew shoulder seams.

3 With RS tog, sew sleeves to joined front and back, placing center of sleeve cap (upper edge) at shoulder seam. Match armhole shaping to sleeve cap shaping.

4 Refold sweater with front and back RS tog. Starting at sleeve hem, sew sleeve seam, cont sewing along side of body to join front and back.

"While swatching, trying to work straight off a ball of rayon gave me fits because the slippery yarn knotted. Thank goodness Nancy Brown came to my rescue. After winding the skeins into balls, she tucked each ball in a plastic sandwich bag and then closed the top with a twist tie so that only the end of the yarn was sticking out."

MARGRET WILLSON, CGOA MEMBER AT LARGE

CHRYSANTHEMUM DREAM

BY JACKIE YOUNG, EXECUTIVE VICE PRESIDENT AND MEMBER OF THE FORT WAYNE CHAPTER IN INDIANA

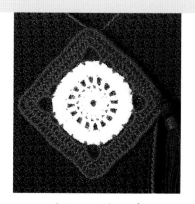

FEATURED STITCHES

Chain (ch); *see page 76*

Chain-space (ch-sp); *see page 80*

Double crochet (dc); *see page 78*

Half double crochet (hdc); *see page 77*

Popcorn; *see page 82*

Single crochet (sc); *see page 77*

Slip stitch (sl st); *see page 77*

Reverse single crochet (rsc); *see page 83*

GAUGE

22 sts and 24 rows to 4" in Grit Stitch pattern

TOOLS AND SUPPLIES

D/3 (3.25 mm) crochet hook size, or size required to achieve gauge

3 large black snaps

2" x 4" thin cardboard

8 stitch markers

PATTERN POINTERS

Not all dynamic sweaters are difficult to make! If you've crocheted a simple afghan or practiced your basic stitches, you have enough experience to tackle this garment.

Some of the shapes aren't the more familiar rectangles and squares, but the shaping and assembly is easy. Each front piece is designed to overlap 2½" at the neck edge. The sleeve has 3 parts: a center panel and a gusset for either side. (See the sleeve assembly diagram on page 65.)

YARN INFORMATION

The sweater is worked in a single yarn. A calm black body is juxtaposed with the cream motif (CC1), which is trimmed in vibrant red (CC2). Jackie designed the garment for CGOA Presents *Frolic* colors #2, #4, and #5. *Frolic* is a lightweight, 100% merino wool—one of the softest and most luxurious natural fibers. Merino wool is springy, so it offers good stitch definition and helps the garment hold its

International style knows no bounds. Move boldly from the office to an elegant evening affair in this dynamic sweater. The chrysanthemum motif ensures that best wishes, good luck, and love will always be yours.

*Colors
MC Black
CC1 Red
CC2 Cream

		SIZE			YARN REQUIREMENTS	
	To fit bust	Finished bust†	Shoulder length	Sleeve length	Body length	Lightweight merino wool MC*	Lightweight merino wool CC1 and CC2*
EXTRA SMALL	31½"	42½"	5½"	17"	20"	2,950 yds. (2,685 m)	200 yds. (182 m) each color
SMALL	34¼"	44½"	6"	17"	20"	3,000 yds. (2,730 m)	200 yds. (182 m) each color
MEDIUM	37¼"	47½"	6¾"	17"	22"	3,400 yds. (3,094 m)	200 yds. (182 m) each color
LARGE	41"	52½"	8"	17"	22"	3,700 yds. (3,367 m)	200 yds. (182 m) each color
FULL FIGURE	43¼"	54½"	8½"	17"	24"	4,200 yds. (3,822 m)	200 yds. (182 m) each color

†*Measurement of buttoned garment*

Chrysanthemum
Dream sweater
shown in CGOA
Presents *Frolic*.

L

GRIT STITCH PATTERN

Multiple of 2 sts + 1 st (also add 2 sts for base ch)

Foundation Row: Dc in 3rd ch from hk (count as sc and dc), *sk next ch, (sc, dc) in next ch*, rep from * to * to last 2 ch, sk next ch, sc in last ch, turn.

Row 2: Ch 1 (do not count as st), (sc, dc) in first sc, *sk next dc, (sc, dc) in next sc*, rep from * to * to last 2 sts (dc and tch), sk next dc, sc in tch, turn.

Row 3: Ch 1 (do not count as st), (sc, dc) in first sc, *sk next dc, (sc, dc) in next sc*, rep from * to * to last 2 sts (dc and sc), sk next dc, sc in sc, turn.

Next Rows: Rep row 3.

shape. However, many other yarns are suitable. Your local yarn shop can offer substitutions, or you can tackle this on your own. Pages 88–89 offer guidance on swapping yarns, and pages 90–91 offer additional information about the CGOA Presents yarn. Suitable replacement yarns for this sweater include Rowan *4 Ply Soft* (100% merino wool) and Jaeger *Matchmaker 4 Ply* (100% super-wash merino wool).

The yardage chart at the bottom of page 61 tells you the amount of yarn that you need for the main color and 2 contrast colors. To determine the number of balls you need, divide the amount required, as listed in this chart, by the yardage on the wrapper of the ball or skein that you have decided to use.

BACK

1 With MC, ch 113 (117, 125, 139, 145).

Row 1 (RS): Dc in 3rd ch from hk, (count as sc and dc), *sk next ch, (sc, dc) in next ch*, rep from * to * to last 2 ch, sk next ch, sc in last ch, turn.

Row 2: Ch 1 (do not count as st), (sc, dc) in first sc, *sk next dc, (sc, dc) in next sc*, rep from * to * to last 2 sts (dc and tch), sk next dc, sc in tch, turn. [111 (115, 123, 137, 143) sts]

Row 3: Ch 1 (do not count as st), (sc, dc) in first sc, *sk next dc, (sc, dc) in next sc*, rep from * to * to last 2 sts (dc and sc), sk next dc, sc in sc, turn.

Grit St pat established.

Work even in Grit St pat (rep step 2) until 20 (20, 22, 22, 24)" from beg. Fasten off.

RIGHT FRONT

1 With MC, ch 71 (73, 77, 85, 87).

2 Work as for Back until 13 (13, 15, 15, 17)" from beg, ending with WS row complete, turn. [69 (71, 75, 83, 85) sts]

NECK SHAPING

3 **Next Row (Dec Row; RS):** Ch 1 (do not count as st), sk first sc and dc, (sc, dc) in next sc, *sk next dc, (sc, dc) in next sc*, rep from * to * to last 2 sts (dc and tch), sk next dc, sc in tch, turn. [67 (69, 73, 81, 83) sts]

Next Row: Ch 1 (do not count as st), (sc, dc) in first sc, *sk next dc, (sc, dc) in next sc*, rep from * to * to last 2 sts (dc and sc), sk next dc, sc in last sc, sk tch, turn.

4 Rep step 3 until 31 (33, 37, 45, 47) sts rem.

5 Work even in Grit St pat until 20 (20, 22, 22, 24)" from beg. Fasten off.

LEFT FRONT

1 Work as for Right Front to Neck Shaping.

2 **Next Row (Dec Row; RS):** Ch 1 (do not count as st), (sc, dc) in first sc, *sk next dc, (sc, dc) in next sc*, rep from * to * to last 2 sts (do not count ch-1 tch as st), sk next dc, sc in next sc, turn. [67 (69, 73, 81, 83) sts]

Next Row: Ch 1 (do not count as st), (sc, dc) in first sc, *sk next dc, (sc, dc) in next sc*, rep from * to * to last 2 sts (dc and sc), sk next dc, sc in last sc, turn.

3 Rep step 2 until 31 (33, 37, 45, 47) sts rem.

4 Work even in Grit St pat until 20 (20, 22, 22, 24)" from beg. Fasten off.

SLEEVE CENTER PANEL *(Make 2)*

1 With MC, ch 69 (69, 73, 73, 79). Place marker on ch to indicate top of sleeve.

2 Work as for Back until 17" from beg. Fasten off. [67 (67, 71, 71, 77) sts]

SLEEVE FRONT GUSSET *(Make 2)*

1 With MC, ch 25 (25, 27, 27, 29). Place marker on ch to indicate top of sleeve.

2 Work as for Back until 1½ (1½, 3, 3, 2)" from beg, ending with WS row complete. [23 (23, 25, 25, 27) sts]

3 **Next Row (Dec Row; RS):** Ch 1 (do not count as st), sk first sc, sk next dc, (sc, dc) in next sc, *sk next dc, (sc, dc) in next sc*, rep from * to * to last 2 sts (dc and sc), sk next dc, sc in sc, turn. [21 (21, 23, 23, 25) sts]

Next Row: Ch 1 (do not count as st), (sc, dc) in first sc, *sk next dc, (sc, dc) in next sc*, rep from * to * to last 2 sts, sk next dc, sc in last sc, turn.

4 Work even in Grit St pat for 8 (8, 6, 6, 6) rows, turn.

5 Rep step 3.

6 Rep steps 4 and 5 until 3 sts rem and side panel is 17" from beg. Fasten off.

SLEEVE BACK GUSSET *(Make 2)*

1 Work as for Sleeve Front Gusset to step 3.

2 **Next Row (Dec Row; RS):** Ch 1 (do not count as st), (sc, dc) in first sc, *sk next dc, (sc, dc) in next sc*, rep from * to * to last 2 sts (dc and sc), turn. Rem sts unworked. [21 (21, 23, 23, 25) sts]

Next Row: As Grit St pat row 3.

3 Work even in Grit St pat for 8 (8, 6, 6, 6) rows, turn.

4 Rep step 2.

5 Rep steps 3 and 4 until 3 sts rem and side panel is 17" from beg. Fasten off.

CHRYSANTHEMUM MOTIF

1 With CC2, ch 6, join with sl st to form ring.

Rnd 1: Ch 3 (count as dc), 15 dc in ring, join with sl st to top of beg ch-3, do not turn. [16 dc]

2 **Rnd 2:** Ch 4 (count as dc and ch-1 sp), (dc, ch 1) in each dc around, join with sl st in 3rd ch of beg ch-4, do not turn. [16 ch-sp]

3 Rnd 3: Ch 3 (count as dc), 2 dc in same st at base of ch-3 tch, popcorn with top of tch and 2 dc (see page 82), ch 1, 3 dc around first ch-sp, join top of first and 3rd dc, *ch 1, popcorn in next dc, ch 1, popcorn in next ch-sp*, rep from * to * around, ch1, join with sl st to top of first popcorn. Fasten off. [32 popcorns]

4 Rnd 4: Join CC1 with sc around any ch-sp, *(ch 4, sk next 2 popcorns, sc around next ch-sp) 3 times, ch 8, sk next 2 popcorns, sc around next ch-sp*, rep from * to * 3 more times, ending last rep with sl st in beg sc, do not turn. [16 ch-sp]

5 Rnd 5: Sl st around first ch-4 sp, ch 2 (count as hdc), 3 hdc in same ch-4 sp, (4 hdc in next ch-4 sp) twice, *(4 hdc, ch 2, 4 hdc) in next ch-8 sp, (4 hdc in next ch-4 sp) 3 times*, rep from * to* around, (4 hdc, ch 2, 4 hdc) in next ch-8 sp, join with sl st to top of beg ch-2, do not turn.

6 Rnd 6: Ch 2 (count as hdc), *hdc in next and each hdc to ch-2 corner, 3 dc in ch-sp*, rep from * to * around, hdc in each rem hdc, join with sl st in top of tch, do not turn.

7 Rnd 7: Ch 1, rsc in each st of rnd. Fasten off.

FINISHING

1 If necessary for your yarn, block each garment piece.

2 With MC, RS tog, and edges matching, sl st to join front to back at both shoulders.

3 Match WS of long edge on a sleeve center panel with a sleeve front gusset. Attach MC with sc at cuff end. Sc along long matched edges to join crocheted pieces. Fasten off. With CC1 and RS facing, rsc in each sc along sleeve seam. Fasten off.

Join sleeve back gusset to rem sleeve edge in same manner. Piece together second sleeve to match.

4 Fold a sleeve in half vertically. Place marker at fold on upper edge. Spread joined front and back on table, RS up. Place sleeve on top, matching stitch marker on upper edge to shoulder seam. Sew sleeve to body.

Join rem sleeve to body in same manner.

5 Refold body and joined sleeves. Join front and back by sewing side and underarm seam. Start at left side seam 3 (3, 3, 4, 4)" above hem (side slit made), sew from hem to armhole, pivot, and cont seam to bottom of sleeve. Sew rem side and sleeve seam in same manner.

SLEEVE EDGING

1 With CC1, sl st in cuff edge, ch 1, rsc around bottom of sleeve, join with sl st in beg rsc, fasten off.

2 Rep edging for rem sleeve.

BODY EDGING

1 **Rnd 1:** With MC and RS facing, join to left front hem with sc. Ch 1, sc along hem, up edge of side slit and down opposite edge to back hem, along back hem and right side slit, and up front, around neckline, and down left front, join with sl st in beg sc. Fasten off.

2 **Rnd 2:** With RS facing, join CC1 to left front edge at hem (bottom corner), ch 1, rsc in first and each sc up front, around neck, and down right front. Fasten off.

SIDE SLIT EDGING

1 With RS facing, join CC1 to left side slit with sl st in corner of back hem. Work 1 row rsc along slit. Fasten off.

2 Rep for rem side slit.

MOTIF

Invisibly sew motif to right front neck edge, matching angle of neck edge to side edge of motif.

CLOSURE

1 Directly behind motif, sew 3 snaps to WS of right front. Position snaps so that right front overlaps left 2½".

2 Sew matching snap halves to corresponding locations on RS of left front.

TASSEL EMBELLISHMENTS

1 Wrap MC around length of cardboard about 30 times. Cut yarn.

2 Thread 6" of MC on blunt tapestry needle. Pull the thread under all of the loops at one end of the cardboard. Remove needle. Pull strand to draw up loops and tie tightly.

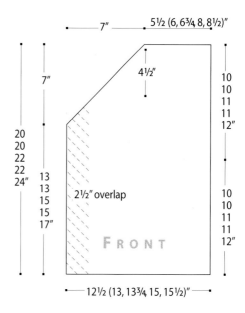

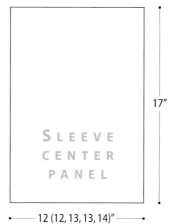

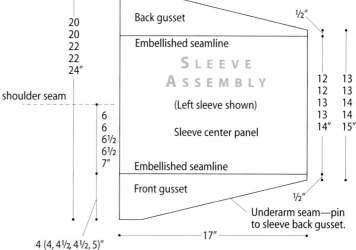

3 Cut loops at opposite end of cardboard.

4 Tightly wind CC1 around loops about ¾" below strand, securing the ends.

5 Make 2 more tassels in the same manner.

6 Sew 1 tassel to the right front edge at corner of motif. Attach 1 tassel to bottom edge (wrist) of each sleeve at wrist.

Sweater stitched by Marion L. Kelly, CGOA member at large

Casual Chic
sweater
shown in
CGOA Presents
Kid Mohair
M Z
and *Graceful.*
F B

CASUAL CHIC

BY NANCY BROWN, MEMBER OF THE
CROCHET GUILD OF PUGET SOUND IN WASHINGTON

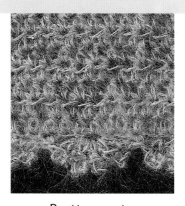

Pretty—not precious—this sweater can survive the rough-and-tumble of everyday living. A stronger yarn is combined with luxury mohair for a kinder, gentler take on the classic sweatshirt.

FEATURED STITCHES

Chain (ch); *see page 76*

Single crochet (sc); *see page 77*

Slip stitch (sl st); *see page 77*

Half double crochet (hdc); *see page 77*

Half double crochet 2 stitches together (hdc2tog); *see page 80*

GAUGE

14 sts and 12 rows to 4" in half double crochet with I/9 (5.5 mm) crochet hook

TOOLS AND SUPPLIES

I/9 (5.5 mm) crochet hook, or size required to achieve gauge

H/8 (5 mm) crochet hook, or size required to achieve gauge

2 stitch markers

PATTERN POINTERS

Aside from the basic working stitches needed to set up and maintain a pattern (chain, slip, single crochet, and half double crochet 2 stitches together), this sweater is worked entirely in 1 stitch. What could be easier? The chain stitch at the beginning of each row is the turning chain. It does not count as a stitch. Traditionally, 2 chain stitches are used for a turning chain that "stands in" for a half double crochet. Nancy uses only 1 chain stitch so that the edges of the crocheted fabric are tidy.

YARN INFORMATION

Nancy has designed a straightforward pattern that is simple enough for a beginner to follow. Nevertheless, she considers it a project for someone with a bit more experience because all of the stitching is done with 2 strands (1 of each yarn) held together and worked as a single strand. CGOA Presents *Graceful* is a fine-weight, loosely twisted, slubbed yarn. CGOA Presents *Kid Mohair* has a fine core and long beard. *Graceful*, in a color called #2 Herbs, brings strength and soft green colors to the fabric while *Kid Mohair*, in #13 Cotton Candy, fills and softens. The single-stitch pattern and basic shaping

	SIZE					YARN REQUIREMENTS	
	To fit bust	Finished bust	Shoulder length	Sleeve length	Back length	Fine-weight mohair	Fine-weight slubbed
EXTRA SMALL	31½"	39"	5¾"	15"	20"	1,600 yds. (1,456 m)	1,600 yds. (1,456 m)
SMALL	34¼"	41"	6¼"	15"	21"	1,600 yds. (1,456 m)	1,600 yds. (1,456 m)
MEDIUM	37¼"	46"	7"	16"	22"	1,600 yds. (1,456 m)	1,600 yds. (1,456 m)
LARGE	41"	49"	7¾"	16"	22½"	1,600 yds. (1,456 m)	1,600 yds. (1,456 m)
FULL FIGURE	43¼"	51½"	8"	17"	22½"	1,800 yds. (1,638 m)	1,800 yds. (1,638 m)

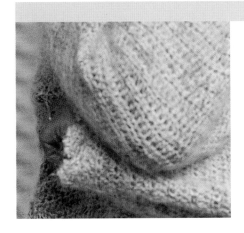

make Casual Chic suitable for many different yarns. For example, you can use Rowan *Kidsilk Haze* (70% kid mohair, 30% silk) and K1 C2 *Doceur et Soie* (70% mohair, 30% silk). For more guidance on swapping yarns, see pages 88–89.

The yardage chart at the bottom of page 67 tells you the amount of yarn that you need for both yarns. To determine the number of skeins, divide the amount required, as listed in this chart, by the yardage on the wrapper of the skein that you have decided to use.

HALF DOUBLE CROCHET PATTERN

Multiple of any number of sts (add 1 st for base ch)

Foundation Row: Hdc in 2nd ch from hk (count as 2 hdc) and in each ch to end, turn.

Row 2: Ch 1 (do not count as st), hdc in first and each st to end, turn.

Next Rows: Rep row 2.

BACK

1 With larger hk and 1 strand of each yarn held tog, ch 69 (73, 81, 87, 91).

   Row 1 (RS): Hdc in 2nd ch from hk (count as hdc) and in each ch to end, turn. [68 (72, 80, 86, 90) sts]

2 **Row 2:** Ch 1 (do not count as st), hdc in first and each st to end, turn. [68 (72, 80, 86, 90) sts]

   Half Double Crochet pat established.

3 Rep step 2 (row 2) until 10½ (11½, 11½, 11½, 11½)" from beg. Place marker at beg and end of this row for sleeve joining.

4 Cont working even until 19¼ (20¼, 21¼, 21¾, 21¾)" from beg or 2 rows (almost ¾") less than desired length, ending with WS row complete, turn.

RIGHT SHOULDER SHAPING

5 **Next Row (Dec Row; RS):** Ch 1 (do not count as st), hdc in first 20 (22, 24, 27, 28) sts, turn.

6 **Next Row (Dec Row):** Ch 1 (do not count as st), hdc in first and each st to end. Fasten off.

LEFT SHOULDER SHAPING

7 With RS facing and working into last full-width row (starting at end of first row of Right Shoulder Shaping), sk 28 (28, 32, 32, 34) sts (bottom of neck), attach yarn with sl st in next st.

8 **Next Row (Dec Row):** Ch 1, hdc in same st, hdc in next and each st to end, turn. [20 (22, 24, 27, 28) sts]

9 **Next Row:** Ch 1 (do not count as st), hdc in first and each st to end. Fasten off.

FRONT

1 Work as for Back until 17 (18, 19, 19½, 19½)" from beg, ending with WS row complete, turn.

LEFT SHOULDER SHAPING

2 **Next Row (Short Row; RS):** Ch 1 (do not count as st), hdc in first 23 (25, 27, 30, 31) sts, turn.

3 **Next Row (Dec Row):** Ch 1, hdc in first st, hdc2tog, hdc in next and each st to end of short row, turn. [22 (24, 26, 29, 30) sts]

   Next Row: Ch 1 (do not count as st), hdc in first and each st to end, turn.

4 Rep step 3 for 2 more times. [20 (22, 24, 27, 28) sts]

5 Work even until same length as back. Fasten off.

RIGHT SHOULDER SHAPING

6 With RS facing and working into last full-width row (starting at end of first row of Right Shoulder Shaping), sk 22 (22, 26, 26, 28) sts (bottom of neck), attach yarn with sl st in next st.

7 **Next Row (Dec Row):** Ch 1 (do not count as st), hdc in same st, hdc in next and each st to end, turn. [23 (25, 27, 30, 31) sts]

8 **Next Row (Dec Row):** Ch 1, hdc in first st, hdc in next and each st across to last 3 sts, hdc2tog, hdc in last st, turn. [22 (24, 26, 29, 30) sts]

   Next Row: Ch 1 (do not count as st), hdc in first and each st to end, turn.

9 Rep step 8 for 2 more times. [20 (22, 24, 27, 28) sts]

10 Work even until same length as left shoulder. Fasten off.

SLEEVE *(Make 2)*

1 With larger hk and 1 strand of each yarn held tog, ch 37 (37, 39, 41, 41).

   Row 1: Hdc in 2nd ch from hk (count as hdc) and in each ch to end, turn. [36 (36, 38, 40, 40) sts]

2 **Row 2:** Ch 1 (do not count as st), hdc in first and each st across, turn.

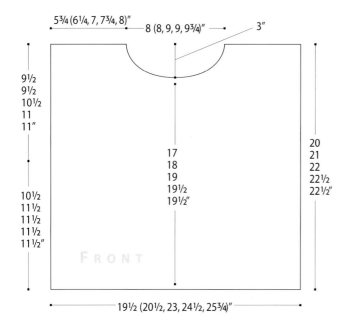

FRONT

5³⁄₄ (6¹⁄₄, 7, 7³⁄₄, 8)"   8 (8, 9, 9, 9³⁄₄)"   3"

9¹⁄₂
9¹⁄₂
10¹⁄₂
11
11"

17
18
19
19¹⁄₂
19¹⁄₂"

20
21
22
22¹⁄₂
22¹⁄₂"

10¹⁄₂
11¹⁄₂
11¹⁄₂
11¹⁄₂
11¹⁄₂"

19¹⁄₂ (20¹⁄₂, 23, 24¹⁄₂, 25³⁄₄)"

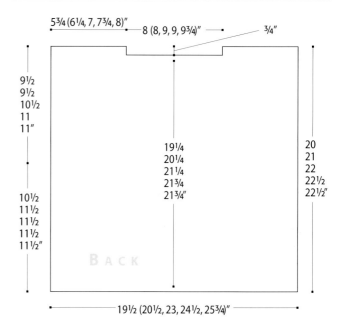

BACK

5³⁄₄ (6¹⁄₄, 7, 7³⁄₄, 8)"   8 (8, 9, 9, 9³⁄₄)"   ³⁄₄"

9¹⁄₂
9¹⁄₂
10¹⁄₂
11
11"

19¹⁄₄
20¹⁄₄
21¹⁄₄
21³⁄₄
21³⁄₄"

20
21
22
22¹⁄₂
22¹⁄₂"

10¹⁄₂
11¹⁄₂
11¹⁄₂
11¹⁄₂
11¹⁄₂"

19¹⁄₂ (20¹⁄₂, 23, 24¹⁄₂, 25³⁄₄)"

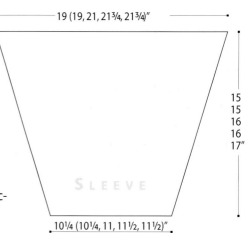

SLEEVE

19 (19, 21, 21³⁄₄, 21³⁄₄)"

15
15
16
16
17"

10¹⁄₄ (10¹⁄₄, 11, 11¹⁄₂, 11¹⁄₂)"

Row 3 (Inc Row): Ch 1, hdc in first st, 2 hdc in next st, hdc in next and each st across to last 2 sts, 2 hdc in next st, hdc in last st, turn. [38 (38, 40, 42, 42) sts]

Rows 4 and 5: Rep step 2 (row 2).

Rep step 3 for 14 (14, 17, 17, 17) more times. [66 (66, 74, 76, 76) sts]

Work even in hdc rows until 15 (15, 16, 16, 17)" from beg. Fasten off.

FINISHING

1 Do not block.

2 With RS tog, sew front to back at both shoulders.

3 With RS tog, sew a sleeve between markers on 1 side of joined front and back. Make sure wide end of sleeve is centered on shoulder seam.

4 Refold body and joined sleeves. Join front and back by sewing left side seam from hem to armhole, pivot, and cont seam to bottom of sleeve. Sew rem side and sleeve seam in same manner.

NECK EDGING

1 With RS facing, smaller hk, and working with 1 strand of each yarn tog to work as a single strand, attach yarn with sc at left shoulder seam.

Rnd 1: Work evenly spaced sc around, working sc2tog as necessary so edge lies flat, join to beg of rnd with sl st in first sc.

2 **Rnd 2:** With larger hk, ch 1, sc in same st, sc in next and each sc around, join to beg of rnd with sl st in first sc.

3 **Rnd 3:** Ch 1, *sk 2 sts, (dc, ch 3, sl st in 3rd ch from hk) 4 times in same st, dc in same st, (picot shell made), sk 2 sts, sc in next st*, rep from * to * around, ending last rep with sl st in beg st. Fasten off.

SLEEVE EDGING

1 With RS facing, larger hk, and working with 1 strand of each yarn tog to work as a single strand, attach yarn with sc at underarm seam.

2 **Rnd 1:** *Sk 1 st, picot shell in next st, sk 1 st, sc in next st*, rep from * to * around, ending last rep with sl st in beg sc. Fasten off.

3 Rep edging for rem sleeve.

HEM EDGING

1 With RS facing, larger hk, and working with 1 strand of each yarn tog to work as a single strand, attach yarn with sc in left side seam.

2 **Rnd 1:** *Sk 2 sts, picot shell in next st, sk 2 sts, sc in next st*, rep from * to * around, ending last rep with sl st in beg sc. Fasten off.

BACK TO

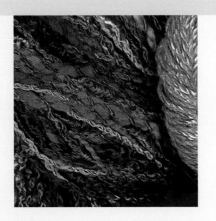

BASICS

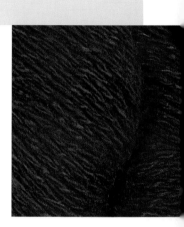

S T A R T - U P   S T R A T E G I E S   F O R   B E G I N N E R S

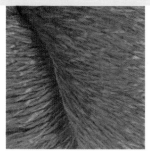

Take steps in the right direction to kick-start your first sweater project. The following instructions will guide you through the entire process. For hands-on guidance, consider attending the next meeting of the CGOA chapter that's near you. (See page 96.)

GET STARTED

1 Pick your sweater. You might want to try the Endless Summer cardigan, the All That Glitters cardigan, or the Northern Lights sweater on pages 16, 24, and 35, respectively.

2 Wrap a tape measure around your body at the fullest part of your bust. Find the closest match in the "To fit bust" column of the size chart at the start of the sweater instructions. This is the size that you will stitch. Photocopy the sweater instructions and then highlight the size you want to make. You'll do more with these pages in a later step.

3 Collect your supplies, tools, and yarn. Remember to include blunt and sharp tapestry needles, scissors, and a tape measure. These aren't listed in "Tools and Supplies" because they're items most stitchers already have in their kits. Consult the yarn requirements chart to determine the amount of yarn you need.

4 You don't have to make your sweater in the yarn—or the color— shown in the photo. "Yarn Information" explains the important attributes of the featured yarn so that you can make an informed decision. There's additional guidance in "Swapping Yarns" on pages 88–89, and your local yarn shop can help you make a good choice.

5 You might want to find out if the yarn shop will wind skeins (the twisted loops of yarn) into balls for you. For a small fee, you'll save yourself a lot of aggravation. Yarn feeding off a hank (or some balls) is unmanageable and may untwist or work into a tight mess as you stitch. Properly wound balls prevent this problem.

PLAN THE GAUGE SWATCH

1 Look at the information under "Gauge" in the project instructions. When you start stitching, the number of stitches and rows that you make in a 4" square should be the same as those noted. If your gauge is different, the sweater won't fit. So it's best to check your gauge by stitching a small square using the recommended yarn and hook size.

2 Note the stitches you need to make your sweater. "Featured Stitches" lists all of them and provides the abbreviations you need to know when reading the instructions.

3 Your sweater will be made with a combination of stitches that's summarized in a stitch pattern near the beginning of the instructions. The pattern consists of a certain number of stitches ("multiple of"). To make the pattern work across a row, you might need a few more stitches ("plus"). Crochet work usually begins with a length of chain stitches into which you work the stitches for your pattern. The number of stitches in your base chain might be greater than the number of stitches needed for the pattern ("add" or "also add"). A 6" swatch is best for testing gauge, so you want the first row of your swatch to have 1½ times as many stitches as noted in the "Gauge" section. Now, if necessary, adjust this number up or down so that it's divisible by the "multiple of" number for the featured stitch pattern. Add any stitches noted with "plus," "add," and "also add."

START STITCHING

1 Make a slip knot on your crochet hook (see page 76). Following the instructions on page 76, make a chain stitch.

2 Continue making chain stitches until you have the number determined in step 3 of "Plan the Gauge Swatch." Now work stitches into the chain by following the instructions for the foundation row of the stitch pattern. You're reading the language of crochet, which is translated in "Abbreviations" on page 87.

3 The foundation row tells you where to place the first stitch. In the Double Crochet pattern in All That Glitters, for example, make the first stitch (a double crochet) in the fourth chain stitch from the hook. Need to learn the stitch? Check it out in "Stitch Primer" that starts on page 76. After you make that first stitch, you might be told that the skipped chains and the first stitch count as a certain number of stitches. In other words, the chain stitches that you skipped might be long enough to be thought of as a single stitch. This is important in subsequent rows.

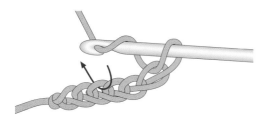

FOLLOW THE INSTRUCTIONS

1 Continue making stitches into the chain according to the instructions in the foundation row. After a few stitches, there's an *. Ignore it until you encounter the second *. The stitches between the 2 *s are repeated the number of times noted in the instructions. On occasion, you may also see stitches inside parentheses. The instructions immediately after the last parenthesis tell you what to do with the

stitches. Frequently, they're all worked into the same stitch.

2 At the end of the foundation row, turn the work so that the opposite side is facing you. Note the direction that you turned it because this should be the same at the end of every row.

BEGIN ROW 2

1 Your first stitch or stitches will probably be chains. They're collectively called the turning chain. It helps you turn the work and "raise" the hook to the height of the first stitch you'll make in row 2. The instructions tell you if this turning chain counts as a stitch, which is usually the case if there's more than 1 chain.

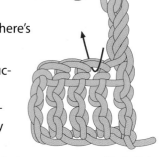

Next stitch

2 Make the stitch noted in the instructions. It will be worked around the top 2 loops of the stitch in the previous row, unless the directions say otherwise. If the turning chain is considered a stitch, then the first stitch you make goes into the top of the second stitch from the end. In crochet language, this is the "next" stitch.

3 Continue making stitches across row 2. If the chain in row 2 counted as a stitch, then the last row 2 stitch is made into the top of the row 1

Turning Chain Counted As a Stitch

Row 4 turning chain

Single crochet

Row 3

Row 3 turning chain

Row 2 turning chain

Row 2

Row 1

Turning chain

Base chain

Chain stitch

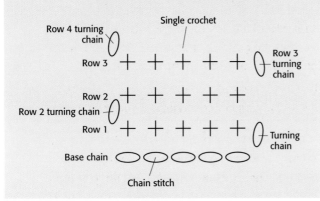

Turning Chain Not Counted As a Stitch

Row 4 turning chain

Single crochet

Row 3

Row 3 turning chain

Row 2

Row 2 turning chain

Row 1

Turning chain

Base chain

Chain stitch

turning chain. If the turning chain in the previous row doesn't count as a stitch, then don't stitch into the top of it. This is important if you want straight edges.

4 Stitch all of the rows in the stitch pattern. If your crocheted fabric square is shy of 6", repeat the specified rows.

5 Fasten off by cutting the working thread, pulling the end through the loop on the hook, and then removing the hook. Tug the end of the yarn to tighten the stitch.

CHECK YOUR GAUGE

1 Place the crocheted square flat on a table and count the number of stitches and rows you made in a 4"-square area in the center of your swatch. If your stitch and row count don't match the gauge in the instructions, you need to make adjustments.

2 If you have too few stitches, make another swatch with a larger hook. If you have too many stitches, try a smaller hook. If the stitches match but the rows aren't exact, you should still be able to make any one of the nice-fitting sweaters in *Today's Crochet*.

PICK YOUR NUMBERS

1 Instructions are given for 5 sizes. Whenever the instructions or numbers apply to all sizes, there's only 1 number. When they differ, you will see 5 numbers. Here's an example: ch 67 (73, 81, 87, 91). The first number, 67, applies to

Extra Small while the remaining numbers, in parentheses, are for the other sizes.

2 On the photocopied pages, use a highlighter pen to mark the numbers that apply to your size. This is a great way to prevent unfortunate mix-ups.

GET AN OVERVIEW

1 A garment consists of several parts: usually a front, back, sleeves, and possibly a collar. There may also be ribbing, cuffs, and a button band, which are usually added later.

2 For a quick idea of where you're headed, look at the garment shapes on the last page of the instructions. Called schematics, they show the overall dimensions of each piece.

STITCH THE FIRST GARMENT PIECE

1 Start with a slip knot on your hook and make the number of chains noted in step 1. Make row 1. The set of numbers in square brackets at the end of the row indicates the number of stitches you should have when row 1 is complete. Look at the number for your size. (It will include the turning chain if it counts as a stitch.)

2 Follow the instructions to the end of the piece. As the crocheted fabric grows, you might want to measure it and compare the dimensions to the schematics. This will identify potential problems before you get too far.

TRANSLATE THE TERMS

1 At some point, you may be told to "work even." This simply means to make another row (or rows, depending on the instructions) with the exact same number of stitches as the last row.

2 Often, "work even" is followed by "in pattern as established." This means that you work the same number of stitches in the new row and continue making the type of stitches that will maintain the stitch pattern that already exists in previous rows.

3 The "next stitch" is the first available stitch, beside the one that you just finished making. The "first stitch" is the stitch that the turning chain is built on.

KEEP GOING

1 Continue making garment pieces in the order that they're listed in the instructions.

2 You'll eventually need to start a new ball of yarn. Switch to a new ball near the edge. When you make the first stitch, merely drop the old yarn and make the first yarnover (wrap the yarn around the hook) with the start of the new ball. Leave about 6" of the new strand hanging at the edge. As your skills develop, you'll learn to work in the loose yarn ends while stitching the rows. For the time being, however, you'll work in the ends when you join the garment pieces.

3 If the garment pieces have similar shapes, the instructions for the second piece might tell you to "Work as for Back." Make the second garment piece following the instructions for the back. In some situations, the pieces may have different shaping at the top, so you will stop following the back instructions at the row specified. "Work as for Back to Armhole Shaping" is a good example. Now the row-by-row instructions for the second garment piece take over.

BLOCK THE SHAPES

1 Blocking gives crocheted fabric memory of the shape you want the garment pieces to hold. Spread each garment piece on a flat surface so that the dimensions match the schematics. You might want to secure them to a cork surface with rustproof T-pins.

2 Some yarns, such as those with a high-polyester content, don't respond to—or are ruined by— blocking. Check the contents noted on the ball wrapper and talk to your local yarn shop. Here are 2 common blocking methods. Whichever method you use, let the fabric dry completely before removing the pins.

Steam: Hold an iron above the crochet fabric and give it a good shot of steam. Don't touch the yarn! Continue steaming the entire shape.

Wet: Rest a damp towel on the garment piece, or spritz it with water and let it sit overnight.

JOIN THE GARMENT PIECES

1 The instructions might specify a joining method. If not, choose from the following.

Running Stitch: Thread a length of yarn on a tapestry needle. With the garment pieces RS tog and the edges even, pull the needle and yarn through both pieces at the beginning of the edges that you're joining. Don't pull through the last 6". Move a short distance along the edge and then pull the needle and thread back through both pieces of the crocheted fabric. Don't pull the thread tight. Continue until the entire seam line is joined.

Slip Stitch or Single Crochet: With the garment pieces RS tog and the edges even, attach the yarn to 1 edge with a slip stitch. Hold the edges together and, working them as a single piece, stitch from the start to the end of the seam line. Working into the end of every row may stretch the edge or make it too stiff. Experiment to determine the best option.

Whip Stitch: Thread a length of yarn on a tapestry needle. With the garment pieces RS tog, the edges even, and starting at the beginning of the edges that you're joining, pull the needle and yarn—from back to front—through both pieces. Don't pull through the last 6". Move a short distance along the edges and then again pull the needle and yarn from back to front through both layers. Don't pull the yarn tight and don't make the stitches too close together. The correct gauge and distance depends on your fabric, so experiment. Continue to the end of the seam line.

2 After joining the pieces, switch to a sharp tapestry needle and weave the ends of the yarn in and out of the wrong side of the stitches in an unobtrusive location. While you're at it, weave in any other loose yarn ends.

Sweaters in *Today's Crochet* are built on a handful of basic stitches that generations have enjoyed creating: slip knot; chain stitch; slip stitch; and single, half double, double, and treble crochet stitches. The following illustrations and steps will guide you through all of these, starting with the simplest. All stitches are shown worked into a base chain, but you can use the same instructions to work the stitches into the previous row of your crocheted fabric.

SLIP KNOT

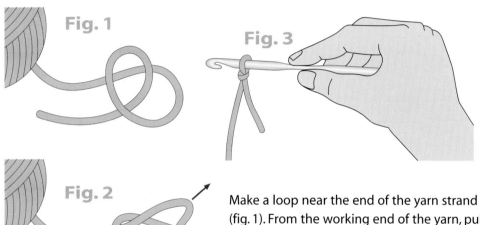

Fig. 1

Fig. 3

Fig. 2

Make a loop near the end of the yarn strand (fig. 1). From the working end of the yarn, pull a loop through the first loop (fig. 2). Place the new loop on the hook and pull the yarn ends to tighten the loop (fig. 3).

CHAIN STITCH

ch

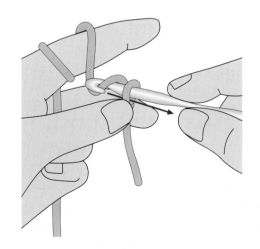

With a slip knot on the hook, wrap the yarn over the hook. Pull the yarn through the slip knot. Lift the slip knot off the hook. Make each subsequent chain in the same manner by wrapping the yarn over the hook and lifting off the existing chain loop (already on the hook).

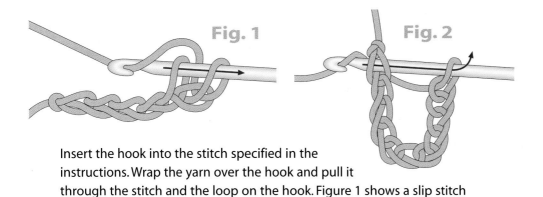

Fig. 1 Fig. 2

SLIP STITCH

sl st

Insert the hook into the stitch specified in the instructions. Wrap the yarn over the hook and pull it through the stitch and the loop on the hook. Figure 1 shows a slip stitch worked into a chain at the start of a row, but you can also make a slip stitch in the first chain in a length (fig. 2), thus creating a round.

SINGLE CROCHET

sc

Insert the hook into the second chain from the hook. Wrap the yarn over the hook and pull it through to the front of the work (fig. 1). Wrap the yarn over the hook again and pull it through the 2 loops on the hook (fig. 2). Finish single crochet (fig. 3).

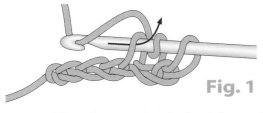

HALF DOUBLE CROCHET

hdc

Wrap the yarn over the hook. Insert the hook in the third chain from the hook. Wrap the yarn over the hook and pull the loop through the chain stitch to the front of the work (fig. 1). Wrap the yarn over the hook again and then pull it through all of the loops on the hook (fig. 2). In subsequent rows, start each half double crochet by inserting the hook in the next stitch, unless the instructions say otherwise.

DOUBLE CROCHET

dc

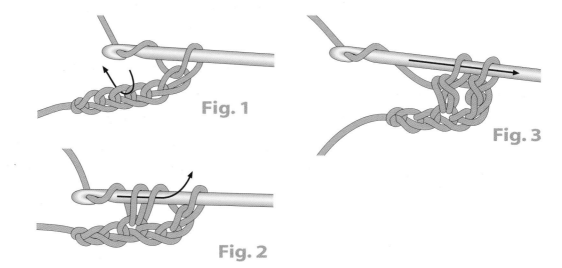

Fig. 1

Fig. 2

Fig. 3

Wrap the yarn over the hook. Insert the hook in the fourth chain from the hook (fig. 1). Wrap the yarn over the hook and pull the loop through the chain stitch to the front of the work. *Wrap the yarn over the hook and pull it through 2 loops on the hook* (fig. 2), repeat from * to * 1 more time (fig. 3). In subsequent rows, start each double crochet by inserting the hook in the next stitch, unless the instructions say otherwise.

TREBLE CROCHET

tr

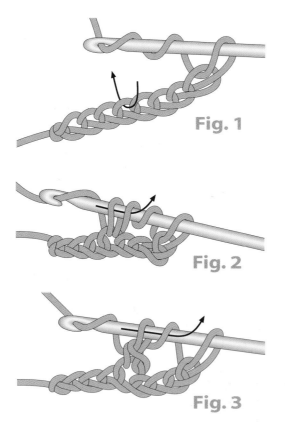

Fig. 1

Fig. 2

Fig. 3

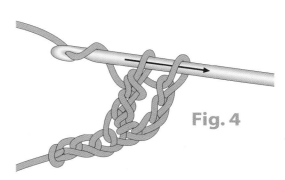

Fig. 4

Wrap the yarn over the hook twice. Insert the hook in the fifth stitch from the hook (fig. 1). Wrap the yarn over the hook and pull the loop through the chain stitch to the front of the work. *Wrap the yarn over the hook and pull it through 2 loops on the hook* (fig. 2), repeat from * to * 2 more times (fig. 3 and fig. 4).

S T I T C H   V A R I A T I O N S

Practically every guild chapter has one or more people who are masters
of stitch variations. While others watch in awe, these artisans bring life
to surface detail, texture, and garment shaping with little more than
variations and combinations of basic stitches. On the following pages,
the variations featured in *Today's Crochet* are explained.

Example: Double crochet stitch in front loop only
(dc in flo)
This variation can be made with any of the basic stitches.
Simply work the usual stitch, but start by inserting
the hook through only one of the loops at
the top of the stitch in the previous row. You
can work into the loop that's closest to you
(the front loop) or the one that's on the back
of the work (the back loop).

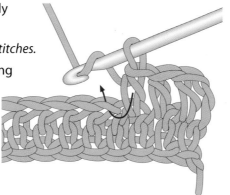

**B A C K
L O O P   O R
F R O N T   L O O P
S T I T C H**

blo OR flo

Example: Back post half double crochet stitch
(BPHDC) into the previous row.
This is working a stitch around the post of a stitch in
the previous row or the row below. It can be made
with any tall stitch, such as the half double, dou-
ble, or treble crochet stitch. The post is worked
from the back, so the posts are recessed on the
right side of the finished work.
Wrap the yarn over the hook. Insert the hook through the work,
from back to front, below the next stitch (to the right of the post
for the next stitch). Swing the hook to the left and bring it to the
back of the work on the opposite side of the post. Wrap the yarn
over the hook, pull the loop to the front, then the back of the
work, and complete the stitch in the usual manner.

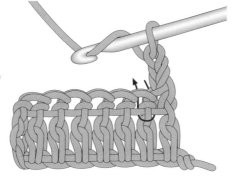

**B A C K
P O S T
S T I T C H**

CHAIN-SPACE

ch-sp

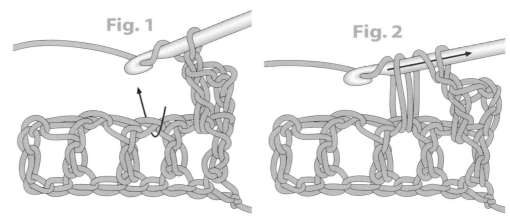

Fig. 1   Fig. 2

Example: Chain-1 space and half double crochet stitch (ch-1, hdc)

A fundamental part of filet and other openwork stitch patterns, the chain-space is simply one or more chain stitches that make a gap in the row. Instructions always specify the process for making a chain-space. In the next row or round, you may need to work a stitch around the chain-space.

In this example, insert the hook from the front to the back of the work underneath the chain—not through it (fig. 1). Wrap the yarn over the hook and pull it to the front of the work (fig. 2). Now complete the stitch.

CROCHET 2 STITCHES TOGETHER

-2tog

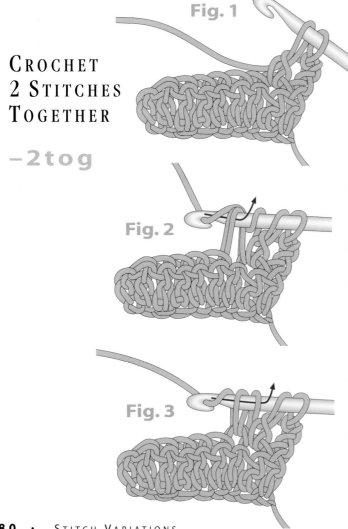

Fig. 1

Fig. 2

Fig. 3

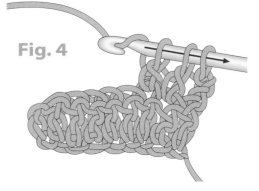

Fig. 4

Example: Double crochet 2 stitches together (dc2tog)

Whether made with single, half double, double, or treble crochet, working two stitches together is an attractive way to decrease two stitches. At the base, it looks like two stitches, but it narrows to a single post at the top. Since it fills the top of both stitches of the previous row, this decrease is nice anywhere along a row or round since there's no gap.

Start the stitch in the usual manner. Wrap the yarn over the hook and insert it into the next stitch. Wrap the yarn over the hook and pull the loop through the stitch to the front of the work. Wrap the yarn over the hook and pull it through 2 loops on the hook (fig. 1). Now begin the decrease. Wrap the yarn over the hook and insert it into the next stitch. Wrap the yarn over the hook and pull the loop through the stitch to the front of the work (fig. 2). Wrap the yarn over the hook and pull it through 2 loops on the hook (fig. 3). Wrap the yarn over the hook and pull it through the remaining 3 loops on the hook (fig. 4).

Example: Front post half double crochet stitch (FPHDC) into the previous row

Just like the back post stitch, a front post stitch is worked around the post of a stitch in a previous row or the row below. The crochet hook starts at the front of the work, so the posts are raised on the right side of the finished work.

Wrap the yarn over the hook. Insert the hook through the work, from front to back, below the next stitch (to the right of the post for the next stitch). Swing the hook to the left and bring it back to the front on the opposite side of the post. Wrap the yarn over the hook, pull the loop to the back, then the front of the work, and complete the stitch in the usual manner.

Example: Linked double crochet stitch (ldc)

Any stitch taller than a single crochet is a candidate for this treatment. Use it when you want a denser, firmer fabric.

Insert the hook through 1 horizontal loop in the middle of the vertical post of the double crochet stitch just made (fig. 1). Wrap the yarn over the hook and pull through a loop (fig. 2). This replaces the first yarn over of a traditional double crochet stitch. Insert the hook into the next stitch in the row or round, wrap the yarn over the hook, and pull it through to the front of the work (fig. 3). The are now 3 loops on the hook. *Wrap the yarn over the hook and pull it through 2 loops on the hook* (fig. 4), repeat from * to * 1 more time.

At the beginning of a row, start with chain 3. To make the first linked double crochet stitch, insert the hook in 1 loop of the second chain from the hook, wrap the yarn over the hook, and pull through a loop. This replaces the first yarn over. Continue as explained above.

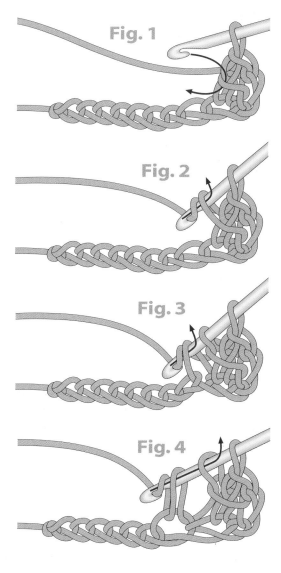

Fig. 1

Fig. 2

Fig. 3

Fig. 4

PICOT STITCH

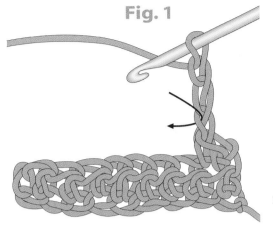

Fig. 1

Fig. 2

Example: Ch-3 picot

This is a tiny bump made by a short length of chain stitches, which is anchored at the beginning and end by two small stitches.

Single crochet in the first or next stitch as specified in the pattern. Chain 3. Slip stitch in the first chain (fig. 1 and fig. 2).

POPCORN STITCH

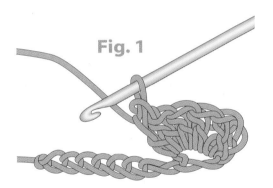

Fig. 1

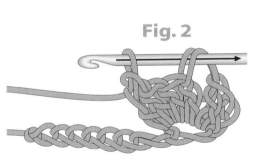

Fig. 2

Fig. 3

Example: 4 double crochet stitches

The raised effect of a popcorn stitch adds texture to a crocheted fabric surface. The most common, shown here, is worked with double crochet stitches.

Working from the right side, in the next stitch make the number of double crochet stitches specified in the instructions (fig. 1). Remove the working loop from your hook. Insert the hook through the top of the first double crochet and reinsert it through the working loop at the top of the last double crochet (fig. 2). Pull the working loop through the top of the first double crochet (on the hook) to close the popcorn (fig. 3).

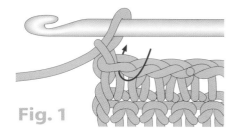

Fig. 1

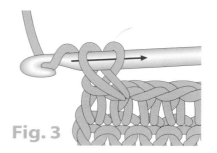

Fig. 3

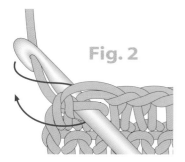

Fig. 2

As the name implies, this is a single crochet worked backward by moving from left to right as you work each reverse single crochet. It's a nice, simple edge finish.

Insert the hook into the stitch to the right, the opposite direction that you usually travel (fig. 1). Wrap the yarn over the hook and pull the loop through the stitch to the right side of the work (fig. 2). Wrap the yarn over the hook and pull it through both loops on the hook (fig. 3).

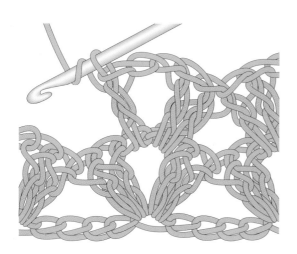

Example: Double crochet and chain shell stitch

Like the popcorn stitch, the shell stitch has several tall stitches worked into one stitch in the previous row. But in the shell stitch, the stitches aren't closed at the top. There are many shell variations, because it's a popular stitch. Often, a chain-space is inserted in the shell, as shown here.

SHELL STITCH

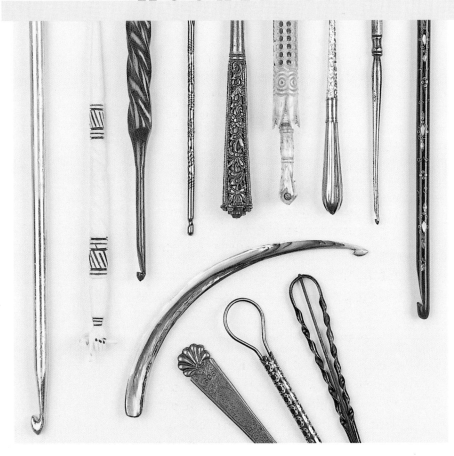

From the warmth of the material to the embellishment and grace of the shape, there's much to admire in this simple tool. Even the most humble version from the local five-and-dime has a sculptural quality.

Beginning crocheters may be lucky enough to receive a complete set of hooks that have a range of sizes. But most will quickly amass more as they learn to work to gauge and use a hook size that's most suitable for yarn chosen for a project. Soon, they'll develop preferences for the shape of the hook and the type of handle.

There are practical reasons for preferring certain hook characteristics: the tip, bowl, and taper at the top of the handle can affect gauge as well as contribute to the stitcher's speed and comfort. Beyond this, however, there's a fascination with shape and beauty. In fact, at this point, it's only a few baby steps to starting a collection of "show" hooks. These hooks are treasured

more for the beauty of the materials and the decorative work than their functionality.

The crochet hooks shown on this page are courtesy of Nancy Nehring, member of the South Bay Crochet Chapter in California. This is a mere sampling of her collection, which tops 2,000 and includes one that's more than 150 years old.

Nancy is a member of the Crochet Guild of America Hook Collectors' Special Interest Group. At least four of the members each have more than 500 "show" hooks. Established in 1999, this group is developing a collection of hooks that will be available for study. They also plan to donate crochet hooks to people in need.

Below are descriptions of Nancy's crochet hooks in the photo on the opposite page, starting with the far-left hook and moving clockwise.

TOP, LEFT TO RIGHT

Boye Aluminum Afghan Hook: This company made afghan hooks in steel (sizes C, E, and F) and aluminum (sizes G and J). The hook was manufactured in 1950.

Hand-Carved Ivory Hook: At the end of the handle, the clenched fist holds a hammer. This piece was created sometime between 1860 and 1870.

Hand-Carved Almond Wood Hook: In 1998, Niles Clark carved the beautiful spiral of this custom-made hook that's made from wood obtained in Nancy's orchard.

Hand-Forged Brass Hook: Also a relatively new piece, this hook was created by Celtic Swan in 1998.

Brass Ormolu (Decorative Mosaic Work) Hook: Look closely and you'll see the aquamarine chips that were set into the end when it was made some time around 1860.

Carved and Pierced Bone Sewing Souvenir: This uniquely shaped piece is a combination crochet hook, needle-case, and novelty. If you peek into the clear center of the fist at the end of the hook, you'll see three illustrations of images of the Sacred Heart cathedral in MontMartre, France. "Souvener de MontMartre" is inscribed on the side. This hook was sold at numerous tourist attractions in the 1870s.

Gold-Plated Crochet Hook: This piece, created around 1870, has interchangeable steel needles.

Early Steel Hook: This is a steel rod lathe turned with a decorative pattern, which was the method used to make crochet hooks before the swaging of steel was developed. Nancy says that this hook was created some time between 1870 and 1880.

Horn Hook Inlaid with Mother of Pearl and Sterling Silver Wire: This exquisite piece has been admired since it's creation sometime between 1870 and 1890.

CENTER

Abalone Hook: The curved shape is natural, because the hook was cut from the lip of an abalone shell in 2000.

BOTTOM, LEFT TO RIGHT

Crochet needles were made up until about 1880. These finer versions of crochet hooks were manufactured like sewing needles, stamped from iron and then converted to low-carbon steel. The following are some examples of crochet needles.

Avery Brass Crochet Needle: Pushing a tab on the opposite side of the handle slides the steel crochet needle into position. Avery made a wide range of decorative brass needlework supply holders. This piece was made between 1880 and 1890.

Sheathed Crochet Needles: This tin lithographed sheath, made between 1870 and 1920, stores three crochet needles. They're hinged to a wire handle. Each needle can be rotated into position for crocheting.

Steel Crochet Needle: The iron handle was twisted into a decorative pattern and then painted some time between 1863 and 1880.

CROCHETERS CAN BE PASSIONATE ABOUT THEIR HOOKS.

HOOK SIZES

What may seem like a relatively straightforward matter—choosing a crochet hook that's suitable for a yarn and the desired gauge—can be a challenge because it's both an art and a science.

PLASTIC, ALUMINUM, AND WOOD HOOKS

U.S.	Metric	U.K.
B/1	2.5	12
C/2	3	11
D/3	3.25	10
E/4	3.5	9
F/5	4	8
G/6	4.25	7
7	4.5	-
H/8	5	6
I/9	5.5	5
J/10	6	4
K/10.5	7	2
L/11	8	-
M/13	9	-
N/15	10	-
P/16	11.5	-
17	13	-
19	15	-
Q	16	-
S	19	-

The starting point is the hook size recommended in the instructions for the project that you intend to stitch. Therein lies the problem. Not all manufacturers have the same standards for hook sizes. In addition, American, British, and metric sizes aren't always exact equivalents.

Consequently, the information in conversion charts such as the one at left don't always agree. A "G" may be listed as a U.S. 7 or 6. In other cases, the U.S. 7 is dropped because it could be confused with a steel size 7 hook, which is much smaller than a U.S. 7 in plastic, aluminum, or wood. An "N" could be listed as a U.S. 13, whereas another manufacturer may jump the N up to a U.S. 15.

The industry is examining ways to solve these problems. In the meantime, use the information in the chart on the next page as a guideline and then trust your gauge swatch to determine the most suitable hook size for your project.

At some point, you need to ignore the numbers on the hooks and simply match the recommended gauge. Once you start creating your own patterns, you'll decide on a suitable hook based merely on the desired appearance of the crocheted fabric. And, if you have developed a taste for handmade crochet hooks (or learned to carve your own at one of Nancy Nehring's classes at the annual CGOA conference) you may learn sooner than most to ignore sizes and use your own judgment.

beg ....begin(ning)

blo ....back loop only

BPDC ....back post double crochet

BPHDC ....back post half double crochet

CC ....contrast color

ch(s) ....chain(s)

ch-sp ....chain-space

cont ....continue(ing)

dc ....double crochet

dc2tog ....double crochet 2 stitches together

dec..............decrease(ing)

flo ....front loop only

foll ....follow(s)(ing)

FPDC ....front post double crochet

FPHDC ....front post half double crochet

FPTR ....front post treble crochet

hdc ....half double crochet

hdc2tog ....half double crochet 2 stitches together

hk ....hook

inc ....increase(ing)

ldc ....linked double crochet

lp(s) ....loop(s)

MC ....main color

pat ....pattern

rem ....remaining

rep ....repeat

rnd(s) ....round(s)

RS ....right side(s)

rsc ....reverse single crochet

sc ....single crochet

sc2tog ....single crochet 2 stitches together

sk ....skip

sl st ....slip stitch

sp(s) ....space(s)

st(s) ....stitch(es)

tch ....turning chain

tog ....together

tr ....treble crochet

WS ....wrong side(s)

YO ....yarn over

Stitching with a recommended yarn isn't always easy—or desirable. In fact, you can end up with a one-of-a-kind garment that's perfect for you if you use a different yarn. The process of choosing a substitute yarn is explained here.

Why rein in your creativity or spend days searching for the exact yarn recommended in your pattern? What if it's discontinued, too expensive, or takes weeks to order? Something in your yarn stash could be suitable. And yarn shops have wonderful selections that just beg to be stitched.

First narrow your choices by identifying yarns that work up to approximately the same gauge. Test gauges on 6" swatches; then measure the stitches and rows over 4".

METERS

X

1.09

=

YARDS

Do not measure from the edges. The base chain, foundation row, and edge stitches are often distorted. Obtaining the gauge over 4" and then dividing by four to obtain the gauge over an inch also ensures accurate information. An exact match isn't necessary. If the gauge of a selected yarn is off by a few rows or stitches, you can always go up one or two hook sizes to get fewer stitches to the inch, or use a smaller hook to increase the number of stitches.

Row gauge isn't as important as stitch gauge. You can always work fewer or more rows to achieve the desired length for your garment pieces. Often, instructions set up the stitch pattern at the beginning of the piece and then tell you to work a specific number of inches. The exception, of course, is areas with shaping. If

SWEATER YARDAGE

÷

YARDAGE ON A SKEIN

=

SKEINS TO BUY

the sweater has shaping over many rows, the row gauge becomes more important.

Don't sway too far off course with the gauge. Changing your hook size won't be enough if the number of stitches to every inch is dramatically different. For example, mohair is fine enough that you could work it with a small hook. But you will be so disappointed with the results! The fabric will be dense and firm.

After you have narrowed your choice to yarns with suitable gauges, you'll probably still have oodles to choose from. Comparing yarn characteristics will help narrow the selection.

Look up the photo of the yarn strand used to stitch the sweaters shown in the photos in this book (see pages 90–91). Now compare your choices to the yarn in the book that matches the sweater you want to make. You can place a length of yarn beside the photo for an accurate comparison, because the strands are shown at their actual size. Even if the gauges are similar, the thickness and other elements of each yarn's personality can be quite different. You want a close match.

Examine the stitch patterns in the sweater instructions. If the garment is worked in a fluffy yarn, the stitch or pattern may look best if you use another fluffy yarn that fills the holes between the stitches in the same manner. You can use a smooth yarn, but the effect will be very different.

Some stitchers choose a replacement by seeking a new yarn with the same content—choosing a 100% cotton if that is what the original instructions specify, for example. This is a safe way to swap yarns, but it's limiting. If the content and gauge are similar to the original, the finished sweater will hang the same. But there are so many other yarns that you can play with.

Different content will work, as long as you understand how it responds when stitched. Think about the yarn's qualities: Is it soft or stiff? Heavy or light? Stretchy or firm? Fluffy or smooth? A metallic—or partially metallic—yarn will be stiffer than a merino wool. A cotton will stretch over time (this can enhance the appeal of the finished sweater, or ruin the fit and stitch) whereas a synthetic will retain the original shape. In fact, a designer may have intended that a sweater only be made with a synthetic, because she is counting on a characteristic built-in stretch, for example.

Color, thank goodness, is mostly up to you. But do keep in mind that some stitches and patterns look best in certain colorways, be they plain, variegated, or space-dyed. (A variegated yarn has more than one color at any point along the strand. Space-dyed yarn is one color at a point and then switches to another color several inches farther along the strand.) If you're unsure how the yarn you have selected will look, the yarn shop owner will probably let you stitch a few rows and inspect the results before you buy.

All that's left is buying the correct amount of yarn. Here's a fast way to figure this out: The yarn chart at the start of the sweater instructions tells you the amount of yardage you need to make a sweater in your size. Divide the total yardage by the yardage

specified on the wrapper of the replacement yarn. The result is the number of balls to buy of the new yarn. It's best to purchase an extra skein because this rough-and-ready yardage estimate isn't exact. Do not purchase a substitute yarn by weight.

If the gauge or the characteristics of the replacement yarn aren't quite the same as the recommended yarn, your starting point for determining yarn amounts is crocheting a swatch in the stitch pattern that is used for the sweater. Measure the size of the finished swatch. Multiply the length by the width to determine the square inches of crocheted fabric. Take a deep breath . . . and rip out your work. Measure the length of yarn that you needed to stitch the swatch. Divide this by the square inches. This is the amount of yarn you need for every square inch of crocheted fabric.

Referring to the schematics for the sweater that you want to make, figure out the square inches of fabric that you need. This is easy for a square: it is simply length times width. You can brush up on your math to calculate the yardage for other shapes or, since most sweater pieces are almost square, just pretend that they are and use the length times width calculation. Total the square inches for all of the shapes—remembering to double the number for sleeves and other pieces that have to be made twice. Multiply the final number by the amount of yarn you need for every square inch of crocheted fabric, as determined by working the swatch.

SWATCH
LENGTH

X

WIDTH

=

SQUARE INCHES
OF FABRIC

LENGTH OF YARN

÷

SQUARE INCHES
OF FABRIC

=

YARN REQUIRED PER
SQUARE INCH
OF FABRIC

YARN GUIDE

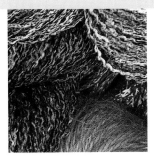

The sweaters shown in this book are made with yarn that's distributed by CGOA Presents (you can order it through the Web site www.CGOApresents.com). For yarn that is space-dyed, multiple strands are shown to illustrate the range of color you will find in a single skein of the colorway used to make the sweater sample shown in the book. The featured yarns are by no means the only ones that will work up nicely for your version of a sweater. The photos of actual-size yarn coupled with the content, gauge, and other information on these pages will help you select an alternate yarn. For additional guidance, see "Swapping Yarns" on page 88.

BLISS

M

52% cotton, 48% rayon; 200 yds. (182 m) per hank
20 sts and 16 rows to 4" in single crochet on an
    E/4 (3.5 mm) crochet hook
Featured in **Northern Lights** (*see page 35*).
To replace this yarn, look for a smooth, medium-twist product that has a slight sheen.

BLITHE

L

50% cotton, 42% rayon, 8% nylon; 200 yds. (182 m)
    per hank
24 sts and 16 rows to 4" in single crochet on a
    C/2 (3 mm) crochet hook
Featured in **English Garden** (*see page 10*), **Strawberry Passion** (*see page 31*), and **Vertical Illusion** (*see page 52*).
To replace this yarn, look for a medium-twist blend of rayon, cotton, and nylon. For the best results, work in a yarn that has a lustrous shine and a soft hand.

CELEBRITY

F

80% wool, 20% viscose; 200 yds. (182 m) per hank
26 sts and 34 rows to 4" in single crochet on a
    C/2 (3 mm) crochet hook
Featured in **Short and Sweet** (*see page 40*).
To replace this yarn, look for a tightly twisted yarn that springs back into shape when tugged gently.

FROLIC

L

100% merino wool; 200 yds. (182 m) per hank
22 sts and 24 rows to 4" in single crochet on a
    D/3 (3.25 mm) crochet hook
Featured in **Chrysanthemum Dream** (*see page 61*).
To replace this yarn, look for a lightweight, medium-twist yarn that has a soft feel.

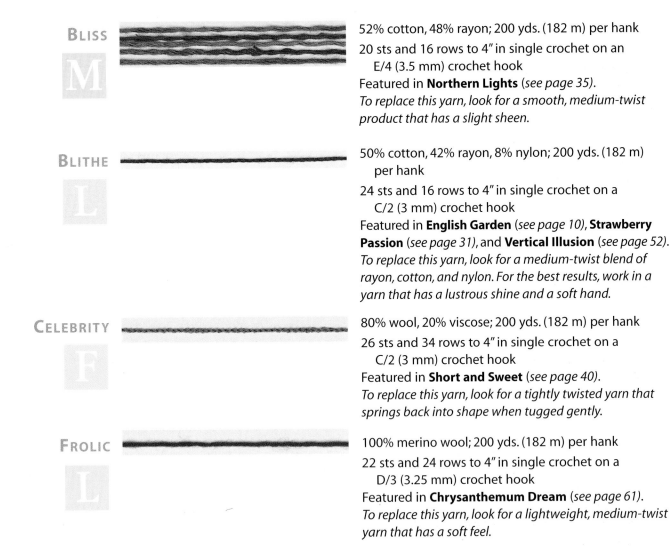

100% rayon; 200 yds. (182 m) per hank

32 sts and 32 rows to 4" in single crochet on a
    D/3 (3.25 mm) crochet hook

Featured in **Casual Chic** (*see page 66*).

*To replace this yarn, look for a loosely twisted,
slubbed yarn.*

GRACEFUL

F

70% kid mohair, 30% nylon; 200 yds. (182 m) per hank

20 sts and 20 rows to 4" in single crochet on a
    F/5 (4 mm) crochet hook

Featured in **Casual Chic** (*see page 66*).

*To replace this yarn, look for another mohair that has a
fine core and long beard.* **Note:** *Kid Mohair is a thin yarn,
but it's classified as a medium-weight yarn. It's best worked
on a larger hook so that the beard has space to fill.*

KID MOHAIR

70% rayon, 30% cotton; 200 yds. (182 m) per hank

16 sts and 16 rows to 4 " in single crochet on an
    H/8 (5 mm) crochet hook

Featured in **The Big Easy** (*see page 46*).

*To replace this yarn, look for a richly textured, loosely
twisted product that has thick slubs.*

RITZ

77% rayon, 15% nylon, 8% metallized polyester;
    200 yds. (182 m) per hank

20 sts and 20 rows to 4" in single crochet on a
    G/6 (4.25 mm) crochet hook

Featured in **All That Glitters** (*see page 24*).

*To replace this yarn, look for a cabled, metallized poly-
ester yarn. It should be flexible enough to stitch, yet firm
enough to hold its shape.*

SPARKLE

100% rayon; 200 yds. (182 m) per hank

20 sts and 20 rows to 4" in single crochet on a
    F/5 (4 mm) crochet hook

Featured in **Fallscape** (*see page 57*).

*To replace this yarn, look for a lightweight, cabled yarn
that has plenty of shine.*

SPLENDOR

L

50% cotton, 50% acrylic; 200 yds. (182 m) per hank

24 sts and 24 rows to 4" in single crochet on an
    E/4 (3.5 mm) crochet hook

Featured in **Endless Summer** (*see page 16*).

*To replace this yarn, look for a lightweight, loosely
twisted blend of cotton and acrylic.*

TROPIC

L

The Crochet Guild of America is a treasure trove of designers, hobbyists, sample makers, and teachers. Unfortunately, not everyone could be included in this book. However, the following biographies of the book's featured designers show the diversity of the CGOA and the many ways that crocheting—and the CGOA—have enriched lives.

Gwen Blakley Kinsler

"As we approach the tenth anniversary of the CGOA, I look back on the path I have taken and where my passion has led me: designer, author, teacher, businesswoman, and friend to hundreds of crocheters. 'Give and you shall receive' rings true for me and I am grateful."

Gwen Blakley Kinsler is an exception—and an exceptional woman. While most designers' skills have been nurtured by family, Gwen picked up the hook at the age of 23, while working as a Peace Corps volunteer in Honduras. This experience was pivotal. It fired her desire to learn all that she could about crochet and build a community of stitchers, as well as taught her to whittle away at difficult tasks. Within a few years of returning to the United States, she founded the Crochet Guild of America.

Gwen's evangelism continues through her coauthored books *Kids Can Do It Crocheting* and *Magical Misers' Purses*. Her crochet patterns and articles have appeared in numerous magazines. Fiber Impressions is Gwen's design business in Rolling Meadows, Illinois. Her Web site is www.crochetqueen.com.

Nancy Brown

"Crocheting is magic . . . with just a few simple tools, supplies, and stitches, beautiful fabric materializes. The design process is exhilarating, and there's much satisfaction working with the CGOA Presents yarns that are chosen specifically with crocheters in mind."

Nancy Brown pursues her crochet with a passion. She recently wrote *The Crocheter's Companion*, plus she publishes a line of patterns and writes continually for magazines. Her patterns have appeared in *Crochet!*, *Crochet Fantasy*, and *McCall's Needlework*.

A long-standing supporter of the CGOA, she has been a vice president and trade-show representative. She operates the CGOA Presents Web site, which offers yarn and patterns suitable for crocheting (www.cgoapresents.com), and is the West Coast representative for the Skacel Collection. You can still find her bestselling *Hat Book* in shops across the country. Nancy lives on the Kitsap Peninsula in Washington.

Jenny King

"The CGOA is my crochet family. Going to the annual conference is just like dying and going to heaven."

Jenny King is one of only a few CGOA members who live in Australia. It's hard to imagine that someone known for stitching beautiful garments started her crochet business publishing patterns for crocheted blankets that keep spectators warm while watching "footy," which is Australian for "rugby." The name of her business? The Footy Rug. Yet crocheted garments have always been a part of Jenny's repertoire. Even as a teen, she was marketing her bathing suits to local shops. She teaches and writes patterns for bead crochet, bikinis, children's clothing, and tartan rugs. Her thirteen books are sold in Australia, Canada, New Zealand, the United Kingdom, and the United States. In all of her publications, she prints her motto: Dedicated to Revitalizing the Art of Crochet.

"CGOA has another meaning for me: Creative Group Of Artisans who share the passion, knowledge, and love of crochet."

MARINKA KODRE-TAYLOR

Marinka Kodre-Taylor is fascinated with the work of human hands, often stopping to observe crafters plying their trade and asking, "What are you making? What is that tool? What are you mixing that with? What is it for? Can you show me? Can you show me? Can you show me?"

Contrary to her mother's assertion that Marinka came into this world with book, hook, and yarn grasped firmly in her chubby little fists, Marinka didn't learn to crochet until she was sixteen years old. Through her first project, a dress made without a pattern, Marinka's grandmother taught her the virtues of a starting chain, the merit of even tension, the visual satisfaction of increasing and decreasing in stitch pattern, and finishing touches that make the difference between handmade and homemade.

Marinka is the Activation Coordinator for Seniors' Services at the Bob Rumball Centre for the Deaf in Toronto, Ontario, Canada. In addition, Marinka sells her patterns through the Web site www.angelfire.com/oh/crochethook.

"This is very exciting and also scary to me. I have been thinking of designing professionally for some time, but it's taken this long to feel confident enough to attempt it!"

DELMA MYERS

Delma Myers is a charter member of the CGOA and a familiar face at the annual conference since its inception. She's had great success with afghans, taking top awards in contests sponsored by the magazines *Quick and Easy Crochet* and *Woman's Day*, as well as the International Crochet Competition.

Is it any surprise that her first project, forty years ago, was an afghan? Too frugal to abandon an unwanted box of yarn and an unfinished granny-square afghan, she taught herself to crochet and hasn't stopped since. Not finding enough sweater patterns suitable for her size and taste, she usually alters existing patterns or designs her own.

Delma, who lives in Anchorage, Alaska, is a Craft Yarn Council of America certified instructor.

"Crocheting is satisfying on so many levels. Through it I can teach, learn from others, and give back to the community."

WILLENA NANTON

Willena Nanton is president of the New York City Guild, Inc. For 27 years, she has been crocheting afghans (using tapestry crochet), baby booties, and sweaters. Her desire to both care—and share—found an outlet in crochet in 1995. The same year that she became a Craft Yarn Council of America certified crochet instructor, she joined an ambitious program to help others. Willena works with a city school to crochet squares that eventually become blankets. At Christmas, these are donated to children living in a homeless shelter. Willena also nurtures new talent by teaching a crochet class for beginners.

"Crochet has been such an important part of my life for a long time. It's a creative outlet, a stress reliever, and a source of extra income. Crochet is also an excuse to get together with other women and talk."

JOY M. PRESCOTT

Joy M. Prescott works backward. No, she stitches in the same direction as the majority of right-handed crocheters. But, while many people have used skills developed in other occupations to launch careers in crochet design, Joy used her pattern instructions to land herself a job as a technical writer.

Back in the mid-'70s, while trolling for salmon off an isolated island in Alaska where she spent most of her life, Joy learned to crochet. Since she started designing in 1980, Joy's patterns have been published in *Crochet World*, *Quick & Easy Crochet* , *Crochet Fantasy*, and other magazines.

Since then, she's made a wide variety of items, but her favorite projects are doilies, dolls, and toys. Now a resident of Redmond, Washington, Joy recently began dabbling in fashion design and freeform crochet.

KATHLEEN STUART

"The CGOA is great for all crocheters because you can learn so much and make many new friends! I have expanded my knowledge of crochet through the conferences and chapter meetings."

Kathleen Stuart loves to crochet afghans, stuffed animals, and toys. One of her "picturesque" afghans (themed pictures worked into the fabric) won the People's Choice Award at the juried exhibit during the 2001 CGOA conference. Kathleen's four children are her best source of inspiration. They even make fun suggestions and sketches for her to try.

Kathleen has crocheted for thirty years, although she didn't start selling her work until about twelve years ago. Her designs have appeared in publications from the Needlecraft Shop, House of White Birches, Leisure Arts, and All American Crafts. She has one leaflet: *Bunch of Beanies*. Her other patterns can be seen in magazines such as *Crochet Digest*, *Crochet Fantasy*, *Crochet Home*, and *Hooked on Crochet!*.

MARGRET WILLSON

"As a member of the CGOA, I feel I have a voice and an opportunity to contribute to an art that is not only my passion and my livelihood, but often my sanity as well!"

Margret Willson, like several other *Today's Crochet* contributors, holds professional member status in the CGOA. As a member of this select group of designers, editors, producers, teachers, and writers, Margret has access to a forum for networking, learning, and sharing information about the crochet business. After 28 years of crocheting, she's still gleaning new tips and techniques from her colleagues.

If you have been crocheting for several years, there's a good chance that you have seen—or possibly made—one of Margret's published projects. Her garments, doilies, and afghans have appeared in leaflets and the following magazines: *Annie's Favorite Crochet*, *Annie's Crochet Newsletter*, *Crochet Home*, *Crochet Home and Holiday*, *Crochet with Heart*, *Hooked on Crochet!*, and *Old-Time Crochet*.

JACKIE YOUNG

"When I first learned to crochet, I had no idea that there were patterns available, so I designed my own sweaters and vests."

Jackie Young lives and breathes crochet. It's her hobby, her passion, and also her business. She's the manager of a local retail yarn shop, Cass Street Depot, in Fort Wayne, Indiana, and has been designing all her life.

You can view her recent work even if you live too far from Fort Wayne to stop by the yarn shop, because Jackie is widely published. Three of her designs are featured in *The Encyclopedia of Crochet*, she is the creator of—and has three designs in—the CGOA pattern line, and coauthored a how-to children's book called *Kids Can Do It Crocheting*.

Jackie was the first chapter development chairperson for the CGOA and the 2000–2003 vice president. Her favorite part about being a member of the CGOA is the interest in crochet that she shares with great friends she's met over the Internet, at the conferences, and the local chapter meetings.

ABOUT THE AUTHOR

SUSAN HUXLEY

"I can't remember a time in my life when I didn't know what a crochet hook was. Raised in a family of stitchers, handwork was part of daily life. My mother, Dorothy Smith, and grandmother, Ruth Gill, gave me a gift that I will never be able to repay."

Susan Huxley is a home-arts publishing specialist who designs garments at her studio in Easton, Pennsylvania. Through her contract publishing business, she creates books, writes magazine articles, and teaches on subjects that are dear to her heart. Visit her Web site, www.SewNTellStudio.com, to find out when she's speaking in your area and to learn new techniques, tips, and inspiration for crocheting, knitting, and garment sewing. You can see more of Susan's work in *Crocheted Sweaters: Simple Stitches, Great Designs*. Susan was the editor of a national Canadian magazine called *Crafts Plus* and a senior editor of sewing books at Rodale, Inc.

ACKNOWLEDGMENTS

The people and companies who worked on or contributed to *Today's Crochet* offered me much more than their experience and skill. Creativity, humor, precision, stamina, and trust are among the many qualities they brought to this project. Meanwhile, garment designers and sample makers scrambled to make sweaters in record time so that we'd have beautiful photographs. (I'd offer kudos to these stitchers, but they'd probably appreciate wrist braces more.)

Today's Crochet is in your hands because Nancy Brown believed in me. This dynamo nurtured the book idea, helped bring it to the Crochet Guild of America (CGOA), and supported me—unquestioningly—at every step.

Guild members submitted more than two hundred sweater ideas when the call for submissions went out. I remember standing in the middle of my studio, surrounded by sketches and swatches spread over every flat surface, thinking, "There's more than a book here. How am I ever going to choose the finalists?" (The proposals were culled to offer a range of style and shaping options, worked in a variety of yarns, to create at least one garment for every season.)

In comparison to some other home-arts groups, the CGOA is relatively small. But the passion and talent of its members dwarfs most other organizations. *Today's Crochet* barely scratches the surface. The CGOA executive deserves my lasting appreciation for allowing me and Martingale to showcase its organization and members.

The sweater designers featured in this book are a delightful group: caring, conscientious, intelligent, and talented. They accepted revisions and eleventh-hour editing with grace and humor. They also listened to me whine about my workload, which proves they also have a lot of patience. In particular, Gwen Blakley Kinsler, Jenny King, and Jackie Young went above and beyond.

Thanks also to Sheila Sait.

When *Today's Crochet* was in development, I was thrilled to learn that Ursula Reikes would be reviewing the sweater instructions. Her keen eye for detail saved my neck.

Thanks also to the Martingale team, particularly publisher Jane Hamada, editorial director Mary Green, design director Stan Green, managing editor Tina Cook, illustrator Laurel Strand, and copy editors Liz McGehee and Ellen Balstad.

My book designer, Barb Field, spent hours developing an understanding of crochet so that she could create a beautiful book. She carefully selected colors to complement the featured sweaters and she took on additional responsibilities.

Robert Gerheart (my husband, business partner, and best friend) had a hand in every part of this book. He took on tasks that varied from the mundane (schlepping boxes to the post office) and sublime (taking the detail photos of the stitching) to the ridiculous (picking oodles of yarn scraps from the fur of our two standard poodles).

The fashion photographs are the work of an excellent team: photographer Kurt Wilson, photography assistant Troy Schnyder, hair and make-up artist Colleen Kubrick, and the models Zora Andrich, Valerie Bittner, Jenny Repko, and Jane Warwick. We had a ball shooting in the Easton, Pennsylvania, home of Sandy and Roger Paul. (Suited more for the wrecking ball in the '70s, they have lovingly brought life back to this grand federal-style building.)

Thanks also to the CGOA for giving me the freedom to make this the best book possible.

CGOA Presents also helped out. Hundreds of hanks went out its doors, free of charge, so that potential designers could develop ideas for particular yarns. And CGOA Presents supplied all of the yarn for the sweaters shown in the photos.

The people and companies mentioned here deserve the credit for everything that is good in this book. On the other hand, it's my responsibility to "get it right," so you can blame me for any errors and omissions that you might find.

SUSAN HUXLEY

THE CROCHET GUILD OF AMERICA
WANTS YOU

JOIN TODAY

ALL ARE WELCOME, FROM NOVICE STITCHERS TO EXPERIENCED DESIGNERS.

CROCHET GUILD OF AMERICA

PO Box 127
Lockport, IL 60441
877-852-9190 (toll free)
www.crochet.org
www.cgoapresents.com

The Crochet Guild of America is a 502c3 not-for-profit organization.

Share your passion for crochet.
Learn more stitches and patterns.
Make new friends.

The Crochet Guild of America is a nonprofit organization of volunteers—people just like you—who want to have fun while preserving and advancing the art of crochet. This group has chapters throughout the United States and Canada, allowing you to spend time with other people who love to stitch.

BENEFITS OF MEMBERSHIP ARE MANY

Crochet! Magazine · Receive a free subscription to this high-quality, bi-monthly publication that showcases fashion crochet and innovative techniques. CGOA members get a special *Chain Link* newsletter insert.

Chain Link Crochet Conference · Enjoy classes, shopping, a juried exhibit, a fashion show, and more at this annual national event.

Biennial Ireland Tour · Explore the rich crochet heritage of this nation with other needlecrafters and fiber enthusiasts.

Charity Projects · Donate to worthwhile projects that help the disadvantaged.

Circulating Library · Borrow publications from the growing collection.

Correspondence Courses · Test your ability and knowledge, and learn new stitches and skills.

Hook Collectors' Special Interest Group · Share your love of decorative, functional, and historic crochet hooks.

Juried Annual Crochet Art Exhibit · Expand your horizons through this unique forum for innovative works that present crochet as a fabric and as a creative construction process.

Master's Certification Course · Enhance your status as a designer or show you're qualified to teach crochet by earning this CGOA designation.

Professional Designation · Network and share product and industry information with other designers, producers, teachers, and writers who are in the business of profiting from crocheting.

CGOA MISSION STATEMENT
To create an environment that will provide education, networking resources, and will set a national standard for the quality, art, and skill of crochet through creative endeavors.